THE FULL ARMOR OF GOD

ARE YOU SURE YOU GOT DRESSED TODAY?

CRISTA CRAWFORD

Planted in Him
Publisher
O'Fallon, Illinois

Let's Stay Connected!
Website: cristacrawford.com
Facebook Page: facebook.com/CCrawfordAuthor
Twitter: @CCrawfordAuthor
Instagram: ccrawfordauthor
Goodreads: bit.ly/cristacrawford

GROUP BIBLE STUDY
SPECIAL PRICING

The Armor of God

The Workbook Companion for The Armor of God

Please email interest to:

books@plantedinhim.com

NEWSLETTER

Sign up to receive a *once a month* newsletter full of updates on new book releases, giveaways, discounts, and encouragement.

cristacrawford.com/newsletter

Copyright © 2016 Crista Crawford.

All rights reserved. This book or parts thereof may not be reproduced in any form, stored in any retrieval system, or transmitted in any form by any means—graphic, electronic, mechanical, photocopy, recording, or otherwise—without prior written permission of the author, except in the case of brief quotations embodied in critical articles and reviews.

Scriptures taken from the Holy Bible, New International Version®, NIV®. Copyright © 1973, 1978, 1984, 2011 by Biblica, Inc.™ Used by permission of Zondervan. All rights reserved worldwide. www.zondervan.com. The "NIV" and "New International Version" are trademarks registered in the United States Patent and Trademark Office by Biblica, Inc.™

GROUP BIBLE STUDY SPECIAL PRICING
The Armor of God + *The Workbook Companion for The Armor of God*

Please email interest to:
books@plantedinhim.com

Planted in Him, Publisher
O'Fallon, Illinois

Because of the dynamic nature of the Internet, any web addresses or links contained in this book may have changed since publication and may no longer be valid.

Any people depicted in stock imagery provided by Thinkstock are models, and such images are being used for illustrative purposes only. Certain stock imagery © Thinkstock.

ISBN: 978-0-9995407-1-8 (sc)
ISBN: 978-0-9995407-2-5 (hc)
ISBN: 978-0-9995407-3-2 (e)

Library of Congress Control Number: 2017960605

www.cristacrawford.com
www.facebook.com/CCrawfordAuthor

CONTENTS

Dedication vii
Acknowledgments ix
Introduction xi
Whirlwind xiii

THE FULL ARMOR OF GOD 1
   Chapter 1 The Naked Truth 3

THE BELT OF TRUTH 13
   Chapter 2 The Most Important Accessory You
   Will Ever Own 15

THE BREASTPLATE OF RIGHTEOUSNESS 29
   Chapter 3 I Feel So Exposed 31

THE SHOES OF PEACE 45
   Chapter 4 My Aching Feet 47

THE SHIELD OF FAITH 61
   Chapter 5 To Shield Or Not Yo Shield? 63

HELMET OF SALVATION 79
   Chapter 6 Always Wear Your Helmet! 81

SWORD OF THE SPIRIT 95
   Chapter 7 "Take That!" 97

THE WAR IS WON 109
   Chapter 8 Are You Dressed For Success? 111

NOTES 123
ABOUT THE AUTHOR 125

DEDICATION

This book is dedicated to my patient and loving husband, Rod, my children who saw the back of my head as I spent countless hours writing at the computer desk, my friends who were my cheerleaders and encouragers throughout this entire process, my parents who are amazing role models, and to all of you who read its pages and answered the call to be fearless warriors of God.

ACKNOWLEDGEMENTS

I would like to thank our children—through blood and through lifelong friendship—for drawing the wonderful illustrations of each piece of armor. I always admired your artistic talents and the special gifts God gave to each one of you. Thank you (from oldest to youngest) Kimmra, Ashley, Mallory, Maddie, Bella, Kelsey, and Abby for using your gifts for His Glory.

INTRODUCTION

While writing *The Full Armor of God*, I was praying over you. My prayer was for God to touch your heart as you read about each piece of His life-transforming armor. When I was in the fifth grade, God told me I would write a book. Last year—at the age of forty-one—He told me it was time. I pray I honor God with my words by honoring you as I talk about His Word. We are living in a world where the dominating theme is pain and worry, and God gave you His armor to fight through the darkness.

Most of my life I battled these forces on my own by discarding God's covering over my shoulder to face my giants alone. After each painful lesson, I started to glimpse the truth that maybe I needed more than my self-will to remain standing. Last year I chose to wear His armor.

His armor of protection is for you to take ahold of. I pray with each piece of armor you wear, you feel God providing you with His wisdom, strength, and courage to battle the enemy who wants nothing more than to derail you from a life fulfilled by Christ.

For each hand that holds this book, I pray the Lord blesses and keeps you and fills you with the life and purpose He has envisioned for you since the beginning of time. Our joy and happiness are gauged by a cultural standard that is counterintuitive to God's standard, and without His armor, it is easy to be deceived into thinking we need less of Him—not more.

If we begin our day without praying to God to dress us in His armor for protection, we might as well be walking out of our front doors naked. Satan doesn't see our carefully cleaned and pressed outfits as we slide into the driver's seat. Our enemy only pays attention to our decision against wearing God's armor which renders us defenseless to the landmines he's carefully planted and expertly camouflaged, so we blindly step onto his battlegrounds.

When God put it on my heart to write about His armor, He made me realize how much of my life I was living without His protection. I ran out of my front door every day wearing only the clothes I put on and never fully dressed myself in what mattered. Satan knows if we make the daily decision to wear the protection of God's armor, it will lead us away from him and toward an eternity with God. God did not leave us sitting ducks in a world temporarily run by Satan. He gave us exactly what we needed to combat our enemy who is trying to drown out the voice of our Father. Your Dad is trying to be heard above the fray. Will you listen?

God gifted you with your unique qualities that in turn gift our world, and He longs to protect your gifts and offer you more joy than you could ever imagine—the gift of love, the gift of grace, the gift of mercy, the gift of forgiveness, the gift of life, the gift of hope, and the gift of peace. This protection is free to us all, but it came at a great cost to God. It cost Him His only Son. Let's go shopping for the right clothes and accessories that will dress us according to His will; the clothes that give us life.

In Christ,
Crista

WHIRLWIND

In a whirlwind I became,
That treacherous gust ripping the plain.
Then midnight struck creating a lamb,
Within the eye of this horrendous sham.
Leery, tired, and dizzy I was,
Horrified, crazed, and lost because
Across the perimeter of this soulless storm
Loomed the other half booming its warn
That once again I will be ripped apart
Unless I offer God my heart
To guide, protect, and love me from this
Shadowed, cold, lifeless twist
Whose knees know no ground to pray
And offers me no light of way,
So, I chose my hand to reach for Him,
Praying that He could stop the winds.
Then the Hand I thought was gone,
Turned my lamb into an immortal fawn.

Crista Crawford

THE FULL ARMOR OF GOD

Finally, be strong in the Lord and in his mighty power. Put on the full armor of God, so that you can take your stand against the devil's schemes. For our struggle is not against flesh and blood, but against the rulers, against the authorities, against the powers of this dark world and against the spiritual forces of evil in the heavenly realms. Therefore put on the full armor of God, so that when the day of evil comes you may be able to stand your ground, and after you have done everything, to stand. (Eph. 6:10–13)

Chapter 1

THE NAKED TRUTH

The week my husband left our family, the dishwasher decided it had a good life and stopped working; my daughter was yelling because a leaking roof caused her painted sky ceiling to form a blue bubble right above her head; carpenter ants graciously announced they were taking up residence in my living room; and I had no clue as to how I was going to afford this house of horrors on just my income.

Have you ever experienced a time in your life when you felt attacked no matter where you turned? Maybe you are experiencing this attack right now. While we choke on the darkness swirling around us, it's easy to feel defenseless and without any hope for relief from this side of heaven's worries and pain. This is a powerful lie Satan has used throughout the ages, and it continues to remain as effective now as it did in the beginning.

Satan is fully equipped with innumerable devices to strengthen our focus on the storms and to shift it away from the promise of the one who can calm our choppy waters. When we feel broken and vulnerable, it's difficult to ignore the trickling whispers chanting, "You are completely and utterly alone." Satan celebrates when we check into the "Isolation Hotel" knowing we will experience an evening of despair and misery. During my windfall of attacks, I may have checked in for one too many nights.

To make matters worse, I couldn't even bring myself to pray. Have you ever been so lost and hurt you couldn't even pray? In my stubbornness, I chose to believe the lie that this season will last forever, and I will always lose at life. These lies crowded out God's truths, and I listened intently. When we believe Satan's lies and stay off our knees, we give him a lot to work with when it comes to burying us neck deep in our feelings of fear and worthlessness. By not taking up God's protection, we hand our peace and joy to Satan on a silver platter.

Two years prior to my husband leaving, I gave my life to Christ. As a new, spirit-filled Christian, I had no problem shouting from the rooftops to anyone willing to listen about my love for Jesus. Shortly after becoming a born-again believer, I experienced my first major storm as a Christian in the form of health issues. I learned quickly how easy it was to praise His name when things were going well, but when my health tanked, my faith and reliance on God tanked along with it.

The body pain, leg twitching, weakness, and exhaustion hit unexpectedly. During this time, I looked around and wondered where my God was. How could this happen to me? I was utterly oblivious to something called *spiritual warfare*, and without God's armor of protection, Satan's lie that God abandoned me seemed believable.

I didn't feel God's closeness as I visited doctor after doctor enduring awful tests that didn't offer conclusive results or a possibility of a little relief. I questioned where God went as I tried to work and be there for my family when all I desperately wanted to do was fall over and sleep. Where was He when I experienced humiliation sitting in a hospital room and listened to the doctors tell me I needed to see a psychiatrist because they couldn't find anything wrong with me? These same doctors kicked me out of the hospital bed even after I told them I had an excruciating headache following the spinal tap they performed. Since the spinal fluid came back clear, they said the procedure was done correctly, and I was being discharged. I cried and threw up from the pain and dizziness as my husband wheeled me through the parking garage, but the hospital didn't care. Where was God then?

Satan doesn't want us to see our world as a battlefield. He relies on manipulation and blindness to this spiritual war so he can collect as many casualties as possible. While we go about our days, unprotected, he uses this time to become an expert student of our lives. He takes inventory of our weaknesses and observes our preferred temptations until he skillfully catalogs what it will take to bring us down. These are the chinks in our armor, if you will. Mine is pride. Satan knew because of my pride I would not have a willing spirit to ask God for help. During this dark patch, he easily disarmed the man-made armor I created for myself which left me no choice but to bow down to the winds that came.

Several days after returning home from the hospital, the pounding headache still hadn't subsided. I couldn't lift my head more than a few inches off the pillow without my stomach churning. My husband convinced me to try another hospital, and the car ride was torturous.

After arriving and throwing up on the registration desk, they quickly escorted me to a room for an evaluation. I'll never forget and am forever thankful for the linebacker-sized orderly who wheeled me into that room. He asked if I could get on the table myself, and all I had the strength to do was shake my head no. I couldn't take my eyes off the floor as I was attempting to force the room to stop spinning. He lifted me straight out of the chair and onto the table like I was a ragdoll. I was so grateful and wanted to tell him so, but all I could offer him was a half-smile.

The doctors at this hospital gave me a blood patch in my spine to stop the spinal fluid leak, and at long last I had relief from the headache. If my husband didn't insist I go to the hospital, I would have laid in my bed forever. Just as I believed the lie that God wasn't with me, I was so beaten down I gave in and started to believe the untruth that there wasn't anything wrong with me. How often in our lives are we willing to believe in the lies despite the evidence telling us otherwise?

During this period, I was hunkered down inside my own sorrow-filled cave with a "Do Not Enter" sign swinging on a nail by the front entrance. I allowed no one to enter—least of all God. I wish I knew about spiritual warfare back then.

Even though I was falling apart, I continued to believe the lie I could handle all of this on my own. Why would I want God's help anyway? I felt abandoned by Him. Have you ever felt abandoned by God? The sad thing is I carried this lie with me into the following year when the second trial took place and my husband left. I found myself not only a single mom—I was a *sick* single mom.

At least at this point I was finally given the diagnosis of Fibromyalgia. I planned out my day because even something as small as buying a gallon of milk was difficult. Sometimes I would sit in the parking lot debating with myself, wondering if today was the day I could make it to the back of the grocery store to get milk for the girls' cereal. Walking a far distance on my bad days was hard because my legs would give out halfway through the store. Each day I was becoming angrier and more frustrated by everything, even the grocery store. Why do they always put the milk in the back?

Over the next several years, God patiently taught me about my pride—the spot that gave Satan a foothold. Satan studied me thoroughly enough to know I liked my independence and self-reliance. I enjoyed telling myself, "Good job!" I tethered my own works to my perceived successes or failures in life.

These weaknesses don't magically disappear when we accept Christ. They continue to remain the chinks in our armor that Satan chooses to exploit. My heavenly Father waited until I was willing to stop the struggle and listen. It's a truth, unfortunately, that took a long time to acquire. I wish I wasn't so hardheaded and learned my lessons the first time, but I am, and I don't. As my beautiful friend Angie explained to me once, we have weeds with long, tangled roots that need to be dug out, and this can take time. If we pull too quickly, we may break off the tops without getting to the roots. We must be patient and let Jesus be our gardener.

So how was Satan so successful in helping me believe the lie? He knew what kind of bait attracted me. And he knows what kind of bait attracts you. A fisherman knows the importance of choosing the right type of food or lure to use as a covering for the true purpose of his hook. The unsuspecting fish must think it's his lucky day coming across a meal suspended out of nowhere. The fish only realizes after the piercing tip of metal snags through his lip that he is in mortal danger, and by that time, it's too late.

Do we know when we wake up in the morning what tempting food is covering our own hooks? Satan knows and plans a menu specifically and individually designed for each one of us. Trial, error, and experience taught us which lures attract which types of fish, and Satan's tackle box is filled and ready to bait my hook and yours.

My bait is pride, but maybe your bait is in the form of an addiction. It doesn't matter to Satan what type of an addiction—drugs, alcohol, sex, gambling, food, pornography, etc.—because he's stocked to bait each one of them.

If your lure is self-doubt and insecurity, he makes you believe you aren't worthy of love, that promotion, or even stepping out in faith and sharing the good news because you think you will make a mess of it anyway.

Maybe you can be snagged with the promise of fortune, so you risk everything on a sure thing, or the fear of failure, so you won't even try.

Is your hook seeking approval from others and having the disease to please? He will pair you with someone difficult while you hold on to the belief you can successfully please that person when everyone knows you never will.

What if you have the opposite ambition and demand respect and admiration from those around you? It's hard to focus on Christ sitting on His throne when we are actively positioning ourselves on our own throne.

Your heart's desire may keep you doggedly working to gain a leg up in the company even at the expense of your family. He makes us believe those long nights away from home missing memories are for everyone's benefit, and not just our own.

What if being second best is never acceptable, and you need to knock down whomever or whatever stands in your way? There are many throne issues—including my pride—repackaged in different ways.

If your bait dangles with what you idolize in the form of money, possessions, or people, then Satan has a plethora of bait to choose from. Television and radio commercials, newspaper ads, and billboard signs help to convince us we need the new latest and greatest product, car, or house if we want to truly be happy. By paying careful attention, we can easily take an inventory of all the ways our desires can bait us.

After our hook is set in our lip and we are suffering the consequences, Satan swiftly turns the tables on us with an accusing finger and asks how we could ever expect a perfect God to love someone as sinful and selfish as us. Satan wants us to believe our fall into temptation is unforgivable, and Jesus didn't die for our terrible sins. He tries to guilt us into thinking we are so past redemption that Jesus excluded our sins as He hung on the cross at Calvary.

Our misguided beliefs keep us isolated and off our knees which is exactly where Satan wants us to remain. In our fallen world, there are endless ways we succumb to sin because no one is immune to temptation. Regardless of what it requires to bait us, Satan waits until we are as trusting and unprotected as that fish now floured, seasoned, fried, and served with coleslaw on someone's dinner plate.

Another common tactic Satan uses is lulling us into feeling comfortable and peaceful in our surroundings as he holds back his traps and snares for a while. This allows us to puff out our chests and murmur to ourselves, "See, it's not so bad. Things are great!" Unfortunately, this too is a trap of sorts. When we don't put on God's armor daily because we believe it's too bulky or unnecessary, Satan has us in his crosshairs, takes aim, and fires.

Pride is something I still struggle with today. I notice when my life is on the upswing, my reliance on God takes a backseat as I once again rush through my day ignoring all the warnings in the Bible about the spiritual battle for my soul and yours. Unless we cover ourselves with the full armor of God, as Paul advises us in Ephesians 6:11, we might as well be naked. That is how Satan sees us—naked and conquerable. God has allowed me to feel the icy wind on my body without His armor. It isn't until I experience the poisonous sting and intense heat of Satan's dart piercing my flesh that I realize too late I morphed into that fish on a hook once again.

We are so lucky our God is a patient, gracious, and forgiving God and intimately knows our struggle. I picture Him lovingly shake His head as we, in a toddler-like fashion, run straight into the peril He is trying to protect us from. It wasn't until another difficult time of attack where once again I was struggling, bedridden with anxiety, and perplexed as to what happened that I came across these words and concentrated on what Paul was trying to say:

> Stand firm then, with the belt of truth buckled around your waist, with the breastplate of righteousness in place, and with your feet fitted with the readiness that comes from the gospel of peace. In addition to all this, take up the shield of faith, with which you can extinguish all the flaming arrows of the evil one. Take the helmet of salvation and the sword of the Spirit, which is the word of God. (Eph. 6:14–17)

Finally, after tripping and falling for the umpteenth time, I opened my heart and allowed this Scripture to seep into my spirit. We have the armor of our Holy God for protection! Why didn't that make sense to me before? You mean we don't have to be skinned and fried every time we get hooked? That addiction, that craving to be admired, the perpetual need to please, and the elusive car, house, or job that never seems to make us happy can bounce off us like we got shot with a Q-tip®? I tested it to see. I taped the Scripture to my bathroom mirror and started to pray each day as I was getting ready for work—focusing on one piece of armor at a time. I was amazed at how quickly those fiery darts were extinguished! I was beginning to experience the strength and power of our mighty God, and my self-reliance slowly started to melt away. Over time it started to become easier to put my faith and trust in Him because His truths were being revealed to me. My eyes began to see.

The Naked Truth

As we immerse ourselves in the Word of God and outfit ourselves with each piece of armor, we grow in the understanding God did not leave us unprotected in this life. Not only did He send His Son to die for us, He sent His Holy Spirit back into the world, so we can clearly hear our Father's voice above the rest. He gave us full body armor to step onto the battlegrounds and win. Let's properly get dressed in the morning and step out of our front doors with boldness and confidence fully dressed in God's love, grace, mercy, and protection.

THE BELT OF TRUTH

Stand firm, then with the belt of truth buckled around your waist. (Eph. 6:14)

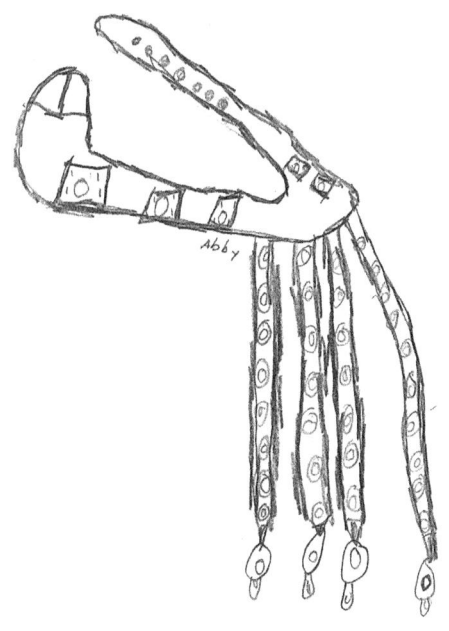

CHAPTER 2
───────────

THE MOST IMPORTANT ACCESSORY YOU WILL EVER OWN

What are the qualities you value in the people within your inner circle? How important are honesty and truthfulness in your friendships, your workplace, and in your spouse? When we are searching for someone to fix our car or take care of a plumbing issue, don't we always want to hear so-and-so is someone you can trust and will give you a fair deal?

When someone is dishonest with us, it is one of the hardest areas to give grace to because our trust is broken. Would you do a business deal again with someone who took your money but didn't provide the service? Would you trust a coworker with private details of your life after they promised they wouldn't spread the previous details around the office but did? Would you try a product again swearing amazing results when it didn't do anything even remotely close to what was advertised? I know I wouldn't.

Truth is what we expect to hear in our politicians, in our government, our schools, in the biographies we read or the *based on a true story* movies we watch, and even the labels claiming a 100 percent guarantee or "free of tree nuts" when our child is deathly allergic to them. Sadly, how often are we disappointed by people and products that didn't live up to the truthfulness that was promised?

In my twenties, I went with a college-sponsored group to Italy. While in Italy, the only thing I wanted to buy was a genuine Italian, leather purse. I searched for a few days until I finally found one I could afford on my income. I loved this purse and for a year, I proudly toted it everywhere. When the leather strap started showing signs of wear, I took my purse to our local leather shop to have it repaired. After inspecting the purse, the shop owner said he would try to mend the strap, but it can sometimes be difficult to sew vinyl. Vinyl! I was completely deflated.

On an excursion to Greece, my parents had a different experience. My mom loves jewelry and wanted to buy a Greek Key necklace. It was toward the end of the trip, and she ran out of pocket money for souvenirs. The storekeeper said she could write a check, but my mom didn't have her checkbook with her. The woman told her to take the necklace—and other items my mom subsequently decided to purchase—back to America and send a check after she arrived home. Now that is trust! She didn't even send my mom home with a bill. She only gave my mom a business card. My parents mailed the check and for the next two years, they received a Christmas card from the shop owner.

Isn't it the best feeling when we meet someone who is exactly like they portray themselves to be, or we use a product that worked exactly as we hoped? Is it me or sometimes does it feel in our current culture this is more the exception than the rule?

I was born too trusting. It's my nature. Are you more of a trusting soul or a born cynic? I remarried a wonderful man who leans more toward viewing things through the lens of skepticism. I could have used him on that trip to Italy because, as embarrassing as it is to admit, I not only bought a vinyl purse, I got duped by a street vendor.

The Belt of Truth

Outside of our hotel I stopped by a crowd of people huddled around a man and a boom box. He had these paper dolls and after rubbing their feet against the speakers, they began to dance! I saw it with my own eyes, so it had to be true! Excitedly, I bought several of the dolls and took them back to my hotel room. Shock and horror set in when I realized I was conned. My dolls wouldn't dance.

Later that afternoon, one of the girls snickered about people falling for the vendor using fishing line to make these dolls dance. I couldn't bring myself to tell her I was one of those suckers. Twenty years later and I'm still left wondering how I allowed myself to be so easily deceived. I'm sure it had a lot to do with the fact I wanted it to be true. Even knowing music coming from a stereo isn't magic and paper dolls don't dance, I wanted it to be true so badly I set aside all logic and reason.

How often are we faced with the truth in our lives only to believe the lie? We have become professionals at convincing ourselves it can't be a lie because it feels too much like the truth. A better job will make me happier; another drink won't hurt anyone. If only I was married, my life would be complete. If only I was divorced, I would feel free. If I try this product, I will be skinnier, or my wrinkles will be gone. God couldn't love me because I've done too many terrible things. I can never be successful or important because of my horrible childhood. I'm in love with someone other than my spouse because we were meant to be together. That promotion will give me the respect I deserve. I can't write a book because no one will read it. What shape does your dancing paper doll take?

Satan loves our insecurities, and he uses them to lead God's sheep astray. I remember learning as a little girl that Jesus is the shepherd, and we are His sheep. It always gave me a warm and fuzzy feeling picturing the image of us snuggled together under the watchful eye of Jesus. Years later I heard a sermon explaining that sheep aren't intelligent animals, and it isn't a compliment when Scripture calls us sheep. I was deeply offended. Then again, I believed in dancing paper dolls.

I heard someone on the radio discussing how much of a follower a sheep is. A herd of sheep on their travels made a wrong turn, and the first sheep went over a precipice and died. Not one, not two, but fourteen of the sheep followed the first sheep to their death. I guess the fifteenth sheep saw the clear string, like my traveling partner did, and thought maybe jumping off the cliff isn't the best of ideas.

Satan is fully aware we are sheep, and he uses cunning, wolf-like methods he's honed over thousands of years to lure us over the edge of that cliff. Without the belt of truth, it will be easy for him to do. Peter warns, "Be alert and of sober mind. Your enemy the devil prowls around like a roaring lion looking for someone to devour" (1 Pet. 5:8). Satan exploits our sheep-like tendencies. It doesn't take much to convince me I can handle things on my own as I run past my Shepherd in the wrong direction. Satan knows what it takes to get me and you there, and we fall for it again and again.

John tells us, "The thief comes only to steal and kill and destroy; I have come that they may have life, and have it to the full" (John 10:10). Darkness vs. light, lies vs. truth, and death vs. life—the choice seems simple, doesn't it? The problem is Satan is so good at repackaging darkness, lies, and death as being truth and life that unless we are armed with God's belt of truth, we will blindly follow all the sheep that fell before.

Have you ever been an outsider looking in at a situation and wondered how the person, couple, or family couldn't see the reality you see? We clearly detect the fishing line that is going to cause a train wreck in their lives, but they appear oblivious to the collision about to take place.

The Belt of Truth

The reason we are sideline witnesses is because Satan isn't interested in covering our own eyes. He is too busy working overtime to make sure the targeted person or family is blind and deaf to the dangers that are coming. Have you ever tried to share with someone what you recognized is going to happen if they continued their chosen path? How did it go? Did they listen? Most of the time the answer is not well and no. I often pray to God to wrap the belt of truth around someone who is struggling and give them ears to clearly hear the truth being spoken into their lives, and He has never let me down.

A friend may call and say, "Hey, you are never going to believe this! My high school sweetheart is in town and wants to meet for coffee. Can I tell my husband I'm going to be with you?"

"Don't tell my wife I bet this month's mortgage payment on the big game. I know I can't lose!"

"I wasn't exactly truthful with my boss about why I wasn't coming in today, but they won't figure it out."

"My kids are good kids. I don't see the problem with them watching whatever they want on TV."

"I was good this whole month, so one drink won't hurt."

"What I search for on the Internet is no one's business but mine."

I wish it was as easy to see our own traps as it is to see someone else's traps. During a two-week struggle with my pride being tested, I realized I needed to know the truth. I work with middle school students, and I head nodded the last couple of weeks to the soft whisper telling me I wasn't good at my job, I wasn't making any difference, so what was the point? I listened to how much I slid in my mothering skills, and after remarrying, I questioned what kind of spouse was I anyway? It was a slow drip of negative whispers that hit me right where it hurts.

My family and my students are for whom I live and breathe and even though my work evaluations, the success of my children, and the love of my husband all pointed to the truth, I gave audience to the lies long enough I started believing they were the truth. These negative thoughts were wearing me down until I taped the armor of God Scripture on my bathroom mirror and prayed the first piece of armor into my life.

"Dear Lord, please clothe me with the belt of truth today. I need to know my value in you and not in the world. What kind of teacher am I? Am I a godly spouse to my husband and a loving mother to my children? What is true, Lord? If there is any worth in me, please let me know. If there are areas in my life I need to improve upon, please let me know that as well. Amen."

I immediately felt the effects of the worry melting off my shoulders. The Lord of all creation was securing me with His truth. He was outfitting me with what He wants me to know and muzzling the lies of the evil one, so I could clearly hear His voice. It freed me to see and accept the smiles on my students' faces. It liberated me to own the loving comments of my husband and sweet embrace of my children. These things would happen whether I prayed that prayer or not. The difference is I believed this truth and not the lie masquerading as the truth. I heard and saw clearly for the first time in weeks.

Satan wants us to be ineffective. He doesn't want us to serve, raise godly children, or have a connected and fulfilling relationship with our family or spouse. Are you listening to the whispers? If so, what lies are you head nodding to?

To hear God's truths, the Bible tells us we need to be firmly planted in His Son. "I am the vine; you are the branches. If you remain in me and I in you, you will bear much fruit; apart from me you can do nothing" (John 15:5). How often are we connected to the vine only to wander until we can no longer see Jesus in our periphery? We jiggle and wiggle on the vine until our branch snaps off and we land on the ground a few, short feet away. Even as our formerly ripe fruit begins to wither and die, and our once flexible branch hardens, we squint up at the vine with our thumbs up telling Jesus, "Don't worry, I've got this!" He peers down at our pathetic state and wonders, "Child, will you ever learn?"

It is similar to us looking at our three-year-old daughter who knows with absolute confidence she can walk the Husky down the street without any help from us, or our sixteen-year-old, newly licensed son who balks against our curfew arguing we must not trust him enough to take care of himself. We shake our heads because we have life's perspective that has given us wisdom about potential future dangers. Jesus shakes His head because He has eternal perspective and knows it's our dependence on Him and not on worldly things that will finally give us the truth and freedom we seek.

To keep us off the vine and away from the truth, Satan wields several effective lies. He convinces many nonbelievers that all Christians are hypocrites. He points out other so-called *Christians* and persuades us to not want to identify as a Christian if it means being anything like that person. If we compare what it means to be a Christian as it looks manifested in life of human beings, it would be like comparing what it means to be a celebrated artist as defined by my dad's Pictionary® drawings.

It is so much fun playing Pictionary® with my dad. When it is his turn to draw, he always tells his partner to, "Think abstractly." We would often get a big chuckle when the time ran out and we compared what he drew to what was listed on the card. He would try to defend his scribbles, but his drawings never even remotely resembled the picture he was asked to draw.

When we think of the term artist, we think of the greats such as Michelangelo, Leonardo da Vinci, and Vincent van Gogh. These are artists that stood the test of time and continue to be celebrated in classrooms across the world. When we dream of becoming an artist, we dream of reaching the heights and celebrity of these artists. When we think of what it means to be a Christian and compare ourselves to each other, it is equivalent to defining what it means to be an artist by using my dad's artistic ability as the measuring stick. Our comparison shouldn't be with each other, but it should be with the greatest Christian who ever lived—Jesus. He is the standard by which we should be comparing and modeling our lives as Christians.

None of us will ever come close to living the life of servanthood, selflessness, and sacrifice that Christ lived—but we are asked to try. Jesus should be our one and only measuring stick. Please don't define what it means to be a Christian based on your neighbor, your relative, or your coworker's life. By doing this, you are comparing the perfect life we are asked to live to humans who will always falter, fail, stumble, and disappoint.

When we fall from grace and someone points at us saying, "If that is what it means to be a Christian, then I don't want to be one," it's like someone pointing at my dad's drawings and saying, "If that is what it means to be an artist, then I don't want to be one." Compare what it means to be a Christian based on Jesus' life. The blessings in our pursuit of Him will come even though not one of us will ever measure up to the perfect life Jesus lived. Your Father isn't asking you to do so to be loved. You are not expected to be the celebrated artist that surpasses the master. Jesus came for the sole purpose of wrapping His arms around our imperfect lives. God then sees us not as we are, but He sees us as perfect and beautiful as His Son.

Another effective lie Satan speaks to keep us off the vine is if God loves us, He wouldn't allow bad things to happen. We decide it is God's fault that we experience pain and suffering.

My parents moved our family from Wisconsin to Illinois when I was in the 7th grade. They couldn't sell their house in Wisconsin, so they reluctantly became landlords to renters living hours away from us. They had two separate renters, and one group was worse than the next. They trashed the house and destroyed a lot of what was inside. My parents didn't call the original architect and builder of their home and complain to them about the situation and demand they fix the problem. Their frustrations were laid at the feet of the people responsible for wrecking their property and altering the house from its original purpose and design.

God's original architecture produced our home in Eden. It was perfect, beautiful, and filled with God's unlimited creativity to bless His creation. When we chose to disobey God, we altered the original purpose and design of our home to become renters in a world now broken and run by a landlord who hates us. We ushered in our sinful world thereby including death and disease into our DNA. Neither of these were in God's original design. We shouldn't blame the architect and designer of Eden for our frustrations but need to lay them at the feet of those responsible for the fall—us.

To fully accept the belt of truth, we must first be willing to acknowledge our need of it. In order to acknowledge our need, we must be prepared to admit to ourselves there is an area of weakness Satan can exploit. If you aren't sure what that area of weakness may be, pray the belt of truth will reveal it to you. Ask God to uncover the areas of your life where you are heeding the lies that are drowning out the truth. Remember, Satan never wants credit for the chaos he creates. Therefore initially sin is an easy pill to swallow. He doesn't want you questioning your desires or evaluating your thoughts because he wants you to believe they originated from you!

Why are we always more willing to believe something negative about ourselves more so than something positive? The answer is we've become so accustomed to the voice telling us the lies—and we've paid audience to the whispers for so long—we can no longer discern its voice from our own. By leaving the house every day for years not fully dressed with God's belt firmly secured around our waist, we inadvertently gave Satan our undivided attention.

The truth you seek may be at the beginning level with questions such as, "God, are you even there? Do you hear me? Do you care about me? Am I as precious as you say I am because I just don't feel it? Did I fall too far away for you to love me? Do I have a purpose? Do I matter?" God will never be surprised or disappointed in our questions. He knows who the author of lies is and how he can skillfully hide the edge of a cliff to make us think it's just another path. God can still reach us even if we already fell over the side. We are His sheep, and He will never leave us even if we believe the lie God isn't there and doesn't care—like I believed.

God doesn't expect us to have all the answers either. His only goal is to foster a personal relationship with us. Please don't accept the lie you must be perfect and sinless to gain God's love. Jesus didn't die for perfect people; he died for us screw-ups. I'm in a place in my life I can confidently lift my hand and admit I'm one of his chief screw-ups who is grateful and humbled by the love and grace He shows me.

As I lay on my side after falling over the edge—yet again—I peer up at my God looking down on me with worried eyes. He asks if I'm okay, cups me in His hands, kisses me on my woolly head, and sets me on the path He originally planned for me. He yearns for me to stay on this path, and I do for a while, until I get hooked again.

The Belt of Truth

The belt of truth is so important. Falling over the edge is terrifying and painful. I'm glad my God's grace and forgiveness are boundless, but I'd prefer not going through this time and time again—wouldn't you?

I'm equally grateful that God did not leave us unprotected, but He did give us a choice: to wear the armor or to not wear the armor. Picture that same strong-willed three-year-old who wanted to walk the dog by herself now having to get ready for a birthday party, and she does not want to put on the dress you bought. Imagine yourself trying to shove this kicking and screaming girl into the frilly dress and never mind the tights you bought to match! What will her demeanor be at the party if she is forced to wear this dress?

God knows our stubbornness, and He is not going to force us to wear His armor. During the time in Eden, it was meant for Adam and Eve to live naked for an eternity. During our earthly time, our nakedness makes us defenseless. It makes us a fish on a hook, a sheep over a cliff, and a branch broken off the vine. God holds out the armor for us to wear but waits for us to willingly step into its protection. I was ready to be properly clothed because solely wearing cotton wasn't helping to win the war for my soul. Only God's armor can do that.

These are a few of the truths I learned since wearing His belt of truth:

- God loves you no matter how far you wandered off. You can't lose His love.

- God never left you. He is waiting nearby for when you are ready to take off Satan's blindfold and see Him.

- Jesus died so we can live an eternity in paradise with our Father.

- This world is temporary. We are made for so much more than just our circumstances.

- God so desperately longs to have a relationship with you that He sacrificed His perfect Son. He allowed His Son to die a horrific death all the while knowing a lot of us won't even care.

- God's original plan included a perfect world. We are the ones who chose this fate, yet how often do we blame God for our pain?

- When we punish the guilty, they live a life behind bars and away from society and freedom. Sometimes they are punished unto death. The Bible says our sin's offense is punishable by death, but our Father chose to take that punishment for us.

- Sin changed our perfect Eden into a broken world. Because God is love and mercy, He still gives us beauty on this planet. He raises the sun to warm us each morning, offers spectacular sunsets to say goodnight, wakes up flowers each spring to color the landscape, and lets us experience love through family, friends, and animals. We keep prisoners in a holding cell when waiting for their sentencing. God gives us the world and waits for us to open our eyes and see how much He loves us.

- God created joy, pleasure, and peace and wants us to experience these during our lifetime. He is not the author of the pain and suffering we endure. We chose to leave Eden the second we decided God's provision wasn't good enough, and we wanted more. We decided it was more important to be all knowing like Him thereby ushering in the knowledge of good and evil.

THE BELT OF TRUTH

- Satan can't stand that God loves us. He hates God and wants to hurt Him, so he attacks those He loves: you and me.

- God created color. He could have created a world only in shades of gray—a world we truly deserve—but He didn't. He gave us the sense of taste, so we can relish in Grandma's food and our favorite restaurant's dishes. He gave us noses to smell our baby's heads and fresh cut grass. He gave us skin that responds to touch, so we can enjoy our spouses caress and the breeze on our faces. He gave us ears to hear, so we can experience every kind of music and the emotions in our loved ones' voices. He gives—and continues to give—endlessly and selflessly to us.

With the belt of truth firmly fastened around our waist, we are cleared to hear the truths God is trying to tell us. What truths does God want you to know? Let's pray the belt of truth into our lives, so we can effectively discern our Father's voice from the one who is trying to drown out His truths.

"Dear heavenly Father, please outfit me with your belt of truth today. It is only by your wisdom and grace I will have a clear path to follow. The truth of your Word, your Son, and your faithfulness is what I want to wear around my waist. By having these, the rest of my armor will have a secure place to fasten. I lived so long without your truths that I am having a hard time hearing your voice and knowing what path you would like me to take. I am ready to clearly hear you speak truth into my life and follow where you are asking me to go. In Jesus' precious name I pray. Amen."

THE BREASTPLATE OF RIGHTEOUSNESS

With the breastplate of righteousness in place. (Eph. 6:14)

CHAPTER 3

I FEEL SO EXPOSED

My daughters mentioned more than once to me their frustrations with Adam and Eve biting into the forbidden fruit that now causes them to have unwanted nights of homework and chores. I simply and honestly replied if it had been Adam and Crista, the results of the fall would still be the same.

It's easy to wag our judgmental fingers at Adam and Eve, but truthfully, we all get snagged by the same means—through our unprotected hearts. You would think having after the fall perspective would better position us because we know there is a spiritual war being waged against our souls. Poor Adam and Eve were clueless. If we know this, why are we still getting snagged today? Apparently, knowledge isn't enough to protect us.

The breastplate of a Roman soldier covers all his major organs for his best chance at coming out alive after battle. It wasn't enough knowing a spear of his enemy puncturing his skin and ripping through his heart would kill him. He knew if he wanted to survive, he needed something stronger than the spear. A craftsman designed a specific piece of impenetrable armor which configured to his torso from materials that transformed those weapons to be something other than their intended death sentence. A soldier knew what was awaiting him on the battlefield, and he protected himself accordingly.

If we understand there is a spiritual battle forged against us, why do we run straight toward the front lines wearing only shorts, t-shirts, and flip-flops? It seems silly, doesn't it? I think the answer lies in how our enemy does battle. We are led to believe we are running toward a beach when it's a desert with cleverly disguised landmines.

Focusing on the mirage Satan has created, it is easy to believe we are not in need of a spiritual covering. He disguises the war zone to look like a normal work or house cleaning day, a few minutes surf on the Internet, a quick drink with a friend, or a casual conversation with that attractive co-worker. There couldn't be any harm looming in these small things, could there be?

His best offense is lulling us into battle with blindfolds and earplugs until the hook is set. How much better off the enemies of Rome would be if the Roman soldiers came to the conflict without their breastplates and bought the illusion the meeting was only to negotiate and not to fight? A surprise attack on an unprotected Roman soldier would be astronomically more successful and efficient as compared to a flat-out, hand-to-hand battle where everyone is fully armed.

Our enemy's only chance of winning depends solely on our lack of protection because he knows the armor will neutralize his deadly intentions. His success is dependent upon us being unsuspecting and unprotected. With God's breastplate, he will fail one hundred percent of the time, and he is more than keenly aware of these odds.

Our spiritual breastplate covers a gift of enormous value. It configures to our torso to protect more than just organs that pump blood or inhale and exhale air. The breastplate of righteousness is crafted by the unblemished blood of our Lord and Savior, Jesus

The Breastplate of Righteousness

Christ, to cover our cleansed hearts. Our spiritual hearts are penetrable in the spiritual realm, and we need an armor that stops the specific types of weapons Satan is aiming straight at our chest. Only when we are wrapped in Christ's righteousness can we defeat the enemy's onslaught of attacks because through Jesus' righteousness, we are made holy, pure, and untouchable. "God made him who had no sin to be sin for us, so that in him we might become the righteousness of God" (2 Cor. 5:21).

Christ is a sinless man that died a sinner's death. He is the only one among us who is truly righteous, yet He died as if He was the sinner. He died a criminal with every one of our crimes written on His body. When we accept Him, we accept our crimes died with Him. When He rose from the dead, we accept we rose up with Him. That is what it means to be born again. "Jesus replied, 'Very truly I tell you, no one can see the kingdom of God unless they are born again'" (John 3:3). Our righteousness came at a steep price, and Satan will do whatever he can to blind us from the importance of the breastplate Jesus selflessly bought for you and for me.

Jesus offers this gift out of His great love for us. When we embrace this gift on the cross, we wear Jesus' righteousness, and our cleansed hearts are beating as one with Christ. Satan is trying to target what Jesus is protecting, and he needs his arrows to have an unobstructed pathway to succeed. Satan desperately wants his arrows to not miss their intended target because when we accept Christ, we accept the call to live a life that resembles Jesus' life. "Then Jesus said to his disciples, 'Whoever wants to be my disciple must deny themselves and take up their cross and follow me'" (Matt. 16:24).

Jesus teaches us to love our enemies, be a servant by figuratively washing the feet of those around us, put our earthly desires last and follow Him, don't covet people or things, and live according to His will. These are a few of the things Jesus calls us to do. I don't know about you, but the first thing that enters my foggy mind when I wake up in the morning is not whose feet can I wash today. My brain usually floods with all the things I need to do to keep my kingdom running smoothly—not God's.

Being Christ-like is not our first instinct, and this is in Satan's favor. He doesn't want our hearts to be searching for ways to be more like Christ. He wants us to be searching for ways to be more like him. With a punctured heart, the Holy Spirit God gave us after we accepted His Son's sacrifice on the cross is drowned out, struggling to be heard. God's voice becomes muffled, and His counsel is no longer at the forefront of our hearts.

If we don't recognize we enter this daily spiritual battle, our focus shifts from God's kingdom to our kingdom as we spend the bulk of our time distracted with the perpetual attacks from the enemy. Our pierced hearts hardwire us to forget our true purpose and leads us to use all our energy on the worries and troubles of a world that is not our forever home.

When you travel out of town and spend a few nights in a hotel room, before you check out are you concerned with the state of the carpet and contemplate whether you should vacuum up the crumbs? Do you worry if the air was left on or wonder if you have enough time to make the beds before you leave? Are you concerned with dusting the furniture or checking the windows to see if they need to be washed? Are you fretting over the house cleaning crew judging you based on the mess your children left in the bathroom?

Most of us don't worry ourselves about the hotel room we most likely will never see again. We are only concerned with gathering up all that is precious to us by checking twice to make sure nothing is left behind. We usually do not give another thought regarding the state of the hotel room once the door is closed.

The Breastplate of Righteousness

Satan wants us to believe our Earth hotel deserves our undivided attention, so we don't attend to what genuinely matters—gathering all that is precious to God by pointing our friends and family to their forever home with Him. In this earthly life, do we ever check twice before we leave to make sure we don't leave anyone behind?

When we wear the breast plate of righteousness, our cleansed hearts keep our focus on what matters and who matters. We have a life span of seventy to eighty years if we are lucky. Even though this is a considerably short amount of time as compared to our eternity, we seem to focus so much more of our attention during our stay here —a place we will leave and never return to—and little time on the forever home Jesus is preparing for us:

> Since, then, you have been raised with Christ, set your hearts on things above, where Christ is, seated at the right hand of God. Set your minds on things above, not on earthly things. For you died, and your life is now hidden with Christ in God. When Christ, who is your life, appears, then you also will appear with him in glory. (Col. 3:1–4)

Jesus protects our hearts. His protection grants us the ability to hear our Lord clearly above the distractions of our lives because these distractions have a way of hording all our attention. He is always with us—and He is always talking—but like a teenager wearing earbuds, we are listening and focusing on the blaring noise of our world and telling God, "Not now, Dad!" If we make the choice to wear the breastplate of Christ's righteousness, the painful and distracting arrows will not hit their intended targets. This affords us the ability to listen to our Father and feel His presence as He holds us in His hands.

Wouldn't you like to know what the God of the universe—the God who created you and loved you even before He sent you here, who celebrated you at your birth and watched over you throughout your entire life, the Lord who is forever present and forever powerful and never leaves your side, the One who is with you in this moment as you hold this book—has to say as you tackle through those tough life decisions? Will you allow Him to bathe you in His peace when your life is rocketing out of control?

How often do we shake our fists at God and wonder where He was during our greatest times of need? This world can leave us feeling empty and alone and with the earbuds firmly in place, we will miss out on the voice of our Dad telling us how much He loves us. "Blessed are those who hunger and thirst for righteousness, for they will be filled" (Matt. 5:6).

What keeps us from extending our arms and putting on Christ's breastplate? Why do we keep in the earbuds and toss the breastplate aside as if it carries little value? What stops us from putting on this armor of protection every single day of our lives?

And how is it we can clearly understand the purpose and value of our underwear more than the righteousness of Jesus? Wouldn't we feel awkward and uncomfortable if we left our homes without putting on a pair of underwear? The thought of the inside of our jeans chaffing our delicate bottoms is enough to make us cringe. Without underwear, we may experience the nagging feeling the world can see through our jeans and notice their absence. We feel exposed without wearing underwear but never feel exposed without wearing Christ's righteousness. Part of the issue is we tend to only miss the things in our life that are familiar.

As a baby, the feeling of a diaper is the only undergarment experience they have, and if that never changed, the diaper would still be their underwear of choice as they grew into an adult. I know

The Breastplate of Righteousness

my girls balked at wearing underwear until they were three years old. They hated the idea of giving up the comfort and security of their diapers.

If I asked them now as a high schooler and a middle schooler to put on a diaper, they would stare at me as if I lost my mind. If we never experienced the joy, freedom, and peace that comes from wearing Christ's righteousness—not ours—we will continue to choose what we have always known. We are so accustomed to feeling the comfort and security of our own righteousness, we never learn the wonderful feeling of wearing the righteousness of our Lord and Savior.

Wearing someone else's righteousness is also countercultural to a world that screams righteousness only has worth if it is self-made, cultivated by our own hands, so we can wear it like a medal around our necks. We are trained in the importance of earning a living and having a good reputation. We attain our diplomas, promotions, and pay raises with hard work. We reap accolades from our bosses and shoulder slaps from our coworkers. We are in a country that prides itself on securing a good life with sweat labor and tenacity. We are told to pull up our bootstraps and get things done.

How often do we look down on people promoted or praised for things they didn't earn? Even our children are taught the importance of work to secure an allowance or play time with a friend. Would you give your son or daughter money for sitting on the couch and watching TV?

The awareness we can't earn righteousness flies in the face of all that's been communicated to us from a young age. Wearing someone else's righteousness is so unfamiliar to us which makes it hard to process. We need to learn to embrace Jesus' righteousness because it must be a daily, conscious decision to put on His breastplate each day. This can be challenging when we live in a world that rewards personal earnings above all else. How often do your hands drop to your sides as you rebuff Christ's gift because you didn't feel like you earned it or deserved it? Satan claps the moment we swallow this lie hook, line, and sinker.

Satan wants us to think we can earn righteousness, but the Bible is clear that we cannot. In fact, Isaiah 64:6 informs us our righteousness is like filthy rags! Those medals we are wearing around our necks are disguised pieces of ripped, smelly socks held together by string and dipped in toilet water. How silly would we look bounding up on stage to receive the medals we earned? Our human eyes look adoringly at the shiny medallions, but when given Christ's eyes, we can see their true worth. Once you are given eyes to see, how fast would you rip that medal from your neck? No matter how good or successful or morally upstanding we think we are, a smelly sock won't stand up to Satan's attacks or help us enter the kingdom of heaven.

Putting on Christ's righteousness would be like wanting to go to your favorite concert, football game, or show, and the tickets for even the cheap seats are way above your pay grade. While standing outside, you are shivering in the cold and looking longingly up at the arena and listening to the *oohs* and *aahs* and joyous clapping when someone comes along and asks if you would like to enter. You answer that you would but explain you don't have the means to go inside. This person asks if you will accept his offer to cover the cost and, while hesitant at first, you make the decision to answer, "Yes!" This man wraps your body in a heated robe, leads you through the gates past the ticket agent, and escorts you to the best seats this venue has to offer. You may initially be in shock as you look around at all the other people and wonder what they were thinking since you didn't earn your seat. You also may be a little

The Breastplate of Righteousness

curious as to what these people did for a living to afford this superb view.

Now imagine in that arena every seat is the best seat in the house, every person is wearing a heated robe, and every person was escorted to the perfect seat by the same man. No one who accepted his offer to cover the cost was turned away. That is what Jesus did for us. If that is all it takes to enter heaven, why aren't we all running to the arena, jumping up and down, waving at Jesus, and gratefully answering, "Yes!" to our need of Him to cover our cost? Why aren't we shoving our arms into that beautiful, warm robe? It may have a lot to do with our need to hang on to the wrong righteousness—our own.

For some, the difficulty in extending our arms to put on His covering is we feel too undeserving to wear Christ's righteousness. We can't shake the feeling we are still wearing that dirty rag under the warrior's covering and worry our dirt and grime will make the breastplate slide right off. We can't accept the truth of Christ's sacrificial cleansing, so we turn away from His offer. This is another tactic Satan uses to keep our hearts exposed.

I'm not a great cook, but I enjoyed making apple pies. To make a good apple pie, the main ingredient should be fresh and crisp. If you leave a cut apple out for even a short period of time, the apple browns and gets mealy, and this makes for a less than appealing dessert. What if I decided to make an apple pie, but I couldn't seem to accept the beautiful, freshly picked apples given to me by a friend. I put my hand up and tell her I don't deserve such apples and send her on her way. What if I insist I use the left-over apples I cut for the pie I made last week because that's what I had in my kitchen? These apples were mine, and I purchased them with the money I earned. I would wind up ruining the new pie I am making because of my unwillingness to accept the offer of the beautiful and perfect gift of my friend.

When we put on Christ's righteousness, we are made new, but we keep trying to apply last weeks, last years, or last decade's sins to what Christ has washed clean because we have trouble accepting His gift of grace. Our inability to let go of what we did earn, whether good or bad, limits our ability to see and accept that Jesus' death on the cross overrides whatever righteousness or unrighteousness we are hanging on to so tightly. "Whoever pursues righteousness and love finds life, prosperity and honor" (Prov. 21:21).

God knew we needed Christ's righteous covering, and He sent His Son for all who are willing to receive Him. We wear the breastplate of Christ's righteousness—not our own—because He is truly the only one who earned it by sacrificing himself on the cross, so we could wear it. We are those awestruck beneficiaries wondering how this could be possible and often believing in the lie that it is not probable.

We do this again and again and continue to wear our own righteousness because we want so badly to see the shiny medallion and not the sock. This leaves our hearts exposed and because of this exposure, our hearts harden, and we turn bitter from the anger at the unfairness of our life's circumstances. We waste all our time building a kingdom in a temporary world that sits on an ever-shifting foundation. Each flaming arrow released by Satan hits its target, and we crumple under the heavy loads we were never meant to carry.

My health issues and broken marriage crippled me because I believed in my works and not Christ's. When my man-made kingdom's foundation was rattled, the whole world fell around me. If I actively wore Christ's righteousness and put my faith and trust in Him, the world around me could fall to the ground, but my

The Breastplate of Righteousness

foundation never would be shaken. I unfortunately picked the wrong righteousness.

Let's talk about objects of this world that we make sure have some form of protection. For instance, where is your jewelry right now? Is it in a jewelry box, shoe box, or drawer? Mine is housed in a sturdy, wooden cabinet stand with hooks for hanging necklaces and drawer dividers for rings and bracelets.

What is covering your cell phone? Is it with or without a case? My case covers the back and sides and has saved my phone from multiple falls.

Is your car in a garage, or is it exposed to the elements day after day? My garage was so full of junk, I had to park outside. Since I'm a person who tends to run late, scraping my car on cold mornings motivated me to clean out that garage and house my car where it belonged.

Do you rent a storage unit or own a shed for those extra items that need a place to go? I passed by a storage company the other day that held their units inside of a building for climate control! Those people must value their items to pay for that extra form of care.

We take such measures to ensure objects in our lives are well protected to avoid having them meet their demise prematurely. A cracked cell phone, lost or stolen jewelry, or a car in need of maintenance can be frustrating and expensive. It's even worse when we took what we thought were the appropriate precautions and measures only to discover they were the wrong ones.

In the ranking of your things, how far up or down the scale is your heart? Besides the clothes that are draping your body right now, what is the spiritual covering you put on before you left today to protect this most precious of your possessions?

Don't be caught at the end of your life protecting it with the wrong means. Attending church, Bible studies, helping people by donating time or money, showing kindness to your neighbor, having honest business dealings, and selflessly taking care of your family are all good things to do in this life. Be careful you aren't tallying them all up and counting your acts of good deeds towards earning righteousness and a pass to enter heaven. Remember, our earnings are like dirty rags. I don't think another bake sale for someone in need is going to cover that cost.

That bake sale should be given out of Christ's righteousness, not to prove how righteous we are. Don't realize too late the protective covering you chose for your heart was the wrong one. That cost will be more than frustrating and expensive. It will force you to miss out on the forever home God has planned. "Ill-gotten treasures have no lasting value, but righteousness delivers from death" (Prov. 10:2).

Out of a purified heart, all the other things will flow. Because we are given grace instead of what we truly earned, we can more easily extend grace to those around us. Without a purified heart, we are locked into the earnings paradigm and it becomes more difficult to extend forgiveness and love to those around us who don't necessarily deserve our grace. Without intimately knowing God's grace, we never truly understand its healing power and in turn, we struggle extending our own.

Along with the belt of truth, let's ask God to cover us with His breastplate of righteousness to protect our cleansed hearts with the impenetrable armor of Jesus. Let's transform Satan's flaming arrows into something other than their intended death sentence.

"Dear Lord, I ask that you cover me today with your breastplate of righteousness. Help me to further your kingdom by tearing down mine and protect me from the enemy who so desperately wants to see me fail. Outfit me with your breastplate and wrap it around my torso so my heart is impenetrable to the enemy's attacks. Help me to seek the comfort and security of the covering of my

The Breastplate of Righteousness

Lord and feel exposed when I step out of His protection. Help me to put my earnings aside and become familiar with the only true righteousness of your Son. Keep my heart protected and pure like Christ's, so I can live a life pleasing to you. Use me to help fulfill your great commission. I love you so much. Amen."

THE SHOES OF PEACE

And with your feet fitted with the readiness that comes from the gospel of peace. (Eph. 6:1)

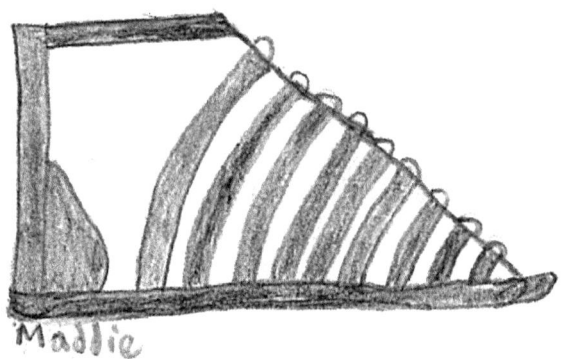

Chapter 4

MY ACHING FEET

Our feet are little antennas for the rest of our body. They let us know if the pool is too cold, the ice is safe to walk on, or the whereabouts of a lost tack. Have you ever stepped barefoot on a Lego®? That feels about the same as stepping on the prongs from an unplugged hair dryer. Both equally procure the familiar step, yelp, and hop scenario.

Our feet are also excellent body thermometers. I can be sweating under the covers but by sticking out one foot, I create a temperature equilibrium throughout my entire body. At the other end of the spectrum, every part of me feels warm, yet my feet resemble the climate in Antarctica.

What about a stubbed toe? That cracking sound when you slam your toe against an immovable object is like no other. Our poor feet get used and abused. I'm sure people with standing occupations—nurses, teachers, and mail carriers to name a few— can attest to how much their feet go through in a day's time. If you have one of these jobs, I can picture many nights at the end of a long workday the couch is as far as you reach before the shoes get ripped off and the rubbing commences.

At the other end of the spectrum, our feet can thankfully produce moments of pleasure. When walking barefoot in the grass, we can distinguish every cool blade kissing and tickling our arches and toes. If you enjoy foot rubs or pedicures, they can transport you into another dimension. My husband's nephew—who loves to hunt and fish and whom I would call a man's man—proudly announced to everyone at his mom's birthday party he had a pedicure. He didn't care if anyone called him a sissy because it was the most amazing experience, and he would do it again!

Maybe you are like me and have extremely ticklish feet. I would give away the world's secrets if someone was holding me down and tickling my feet. During my first massage, the lights were dim, the soft music was covering me, and incense swirled in the air. The atmosphere was warm, relaxing, and if allowed, I could have napped there for hours. When the masseuse's expert touch transitioned from my legs to my feet, I jerked and burst out laughing—scaring her half to death. She wasn't pleased with me, and I received a well-deserved etiquette lesson on how important it is to inform the therapist next time of my sensitive feet to avoid another disruption. Oops!

How much attention do you pay toward your feet? If we peeked inside your closet right now, how many pairs of shoes and boots would stare back at us? Does your system of organization allow for easy access to all your shoes, or do you reach into the jumbled mess, pull out a pair, and hope for the best? Are there shoes for every occasion or one pair will do? A personality survey could easily be created on each one of us focusing exclusively on our shoe buying habits.

It also doesn't hurt that shoe stores are almost limitless on what they can offer a customer. It's not a plain pair of sneakers anymore. This is by no means an exhaustive list, but here are some of the categories that keep us perusing the aisles of the shoe stores: basketball, football, volleyball, tennis, soccer, and wrestling shoes,

The Shoes of Peace

track and field shoes—ones with spikes and ones without—ballet, tap, and jazz shoes, golf, aerobic, and bicycling shoes, running, jogging, walking and cross country shoes, business shoes, work boots, clogs, flip-flops, sandals, wedges, wedding shoes, dyeable shoes, high heels, low heels, stilettos, open-toe and closed-toe shoes, slip-ons, wing-tipped, loafers, dress shoes, flats, shoes with Velcro®, zippers, or laces, cowboy boots, riding boots, combat boots, snow and rain boots, galoshes, thigh-high or moto boots, chunky or low heeled boots, leather, vinyl, gel-lined or fur-lined, not to mention the variety of slippers to choose from. This is the tip of the iceberg of our choices in this country, and those variables skyrocket when factoring in colors and price ranges.

I came across a statistic that concluded the United States spends over twenty-nine billion dollars on shoes annually.[1] To represent this number, I found a website that gave a wonderful illustration. For a person to walk one billion steps, they would have to walk 15.278 times around the equator.[2] Now multiply that number by twenty-nine, and that is how much money we spend on shoes annually! As a country, we have an obvious love affair with our feet.

After we purchase the shoes and wear them, we inadvertently create little advertisements about ourselves right on our feet. If we were to look down at each other's feet and not at the rest of our bodies, we could easily make some assumptions about each other by simply observing each other's footwear. We can identify who plays sports, who dresses for comfort, who is fighting for our country or within our community, who works outdoors and who works indoors, who works at certain jobs from nurses to businessmen, men from women, ranchers from city folks, dancers and beach-goers, women who feel at home with a heel and those who prefer flats, people who are budget shoppers or extravagant spenders, and the list goes on and on.

Let's be honest, how often do you look at the feet of the person you are talking to, passing by, or standing next to on an elevator and check out their footwear? Do you think to yourself, "Those look cute," "He must be successful," or "Why would they wear those shoes with that outfit?" I work in a middle school and a huge chunk of the students' conversation revolves around what is on their feet.

When we do choose a shoe for a specific function and not for fashion, a lot of care and research is usually involved which will culminate in multiple shoe fittings and store hopping. When someone is running a full marathon, the last thing they want to worry about are blisters or painful arches. For this reason, they wouldn't be looking for wedges or cowboy boots and would bypass those aisles to search for shoes specifically created for running. They need to find shoes that fit and support their feet so perfectly, they wouldn't even notice they were wearing them. Ultimately, runners choose the right shoe, so they can go the distance.

When entering a spiritual battle, Satan would invariably look down at our feet. He would want to know if we came to the battle fully prepared, or if he could easily make us stumble with little effort on his part. He takes note of whether we are walking in the shoes of peace which are designed and created by the good news of the death and resurrection of Jesus. If we decided against getting properly dressed in Christ's shoes, our enemy knows that it won't take much for us to collapse into the dirt. We are asked to be the hands and feet of Christ while on Earth, and for us to do this, we need to walk across the whole distance of life's minefields with our joy and peace intact. Only Christ's shoes are capable of such an amazing feat, and our feet desperately need His shoes if we are to run this marathon of life.

The Shoes of Peace

Is it possible for a soldier to maintain eye contact with the enemy while running onto the battlefield barefoot? Probably not. The soldier would be forced to constantly scan the ground to avoid rocks, holes, and debris. Their footing would be unsure, and instincts would cause him or her to look away to avoid a sprained ankle or cut sole. How fearless or bold would the soldier look high stepping across the battlefield muttering, "Ow, ow, ow, ow!" Without Christ's shoes, we are oblivious to Satan's plans because we are so consumed with the worries on the ground, we ignore what is coming on the horizon. We walk through life unaware because we are high-stepping and blind to the attacks he has planned.

Jesus did not promise an easy life on Earth and wearing the shoes of peace won't take away the landmines from our human experience. We will always have rocks, holes, and debris along our path until we are reunited with our Father. Jesus did promise He is always with us. He will carry us through these rough times and unimaginably we can even feel joy! In John 16:33, Jesus says, "I have told you these things, so that in me you may have peace. In this world you will have trouble. But take heart! I have overcome the world."

Knowing the battlefield is there, if we choose to wear footwear ill-fitting for the type of battles we encounter, we will not be looking ahead but down and away from our Father who wants to guide us through the chaos. Jesus did tell us if we took our burdens and concerns to Him, He would lean down and slip our feet into His perfect peace. The shoes of peace give us the freedom to step out courageously, with self-assuredness, and without worry or fear. These shoes fit so perfectly that when we walk, we almost hover above our circumstances.

Those obstacles, challenges, and difficulties in our way are no longer making us stumble and fall. The shoes of peace provide a light instep cushioned with the love of Jesus who bore all our sins on the cross. He took the death penalty for us, so we now can take heart and feel joy knowing our pain and suffering has an expiration date.

The gospel gives us the courage to step out because any pain, sadness, hurt, fear, worry, depression, and even death has already been conquered. The spiritual war is already won by our Lord and Savior and this earthly battlefield is not our final resting place. While we are here, Philippians 4:6–7 tells us, "Do not be anxious about anything, but in every situation, by prayer and petition, with thanksgiving, present your requests to God. And the peace of God, which transcends all understanding, will guard your hearts and your minds in Christ Jesus."

What shoes you choose, whether store bought or Christ bought, will determine if you step out each day scanning the ground for potential pitfalls or looking straight ahead with the confidence you are walking in Christ's peace.

This brings to mind those movies where the heroic figure is walking in slow motion down a decimated street with buildings and cars exploding on either side of him, yet he doesn't even flinch. He keeps moving forward with his eyes locked directly on his enemy. He has no fear how this battle will end because he confidently knows victory is his. Cue the music. Don't you love those parts of the movie?

The truth is we are living that movie. Instead of cars and buildings exploding, how many of your friends or family members lives blew up because they fell into temptation? How many times has your body been slammed against the wall from a blast because you followed a path you were never meant to take? Instead of walking with sure steps, do you, or someone you know, close your eyes and run blindly into the fray hoping for the best? I know I've

The Shoes of Peace

perfected the *duck and move* technique while going through my personal battles. It makes it difficult to see clearly where we need to go, let alone help anyone else along the way, when we are forced to cover our heads from the falling wreckage of our lives.

God never intended for us to duck and move or cover our heads as we walk blindly into an abyss. If He wanted us to live without peace and hope, He would have rescued His Son from meeting such an unfair and painful death. God easily could lift His hands and declare, "Since you allowed sin to enter into this world, you need to figure out how to deal with it!" Thankfully, God's response to our plight is one of love and not frustration. He answered by gifting us with the gospel of peace and allowed His Son to die. He had to die, so our sins could die with Him. He raised to life and we can too when we choose to die to ourselves and accept the gift He offers.

Too often, unfortunately, we don't live like Christ's peace even exists, or that His death even matters. We view it as some historical fact that has little to do with our present circumstances. Even if we do believe His death has meaning, how often do we throw off His shoes of peace and stick our feet into the flip-flops because we don't trust in Jesus' ability to provide the hope and peace He promised? We may give into the lie He is not enough to keep us safely above the molten lava outpouring from our hurting lives. I purchased and worn these flip-flops in many colors and styles during my lifetime. Have you?

By not wearing Christ's shoes of peace, I panicked through most of my storms with little movement forward. I huddled in fear and remained stagnant until the trials passed. Because I did this so often, I can relate to the Bible story where Peter steps out from the boat to meet Jesus and quickly surrenders to the fear of his surroundings. He shifted focus from gazing straight into the eyes of his Savior to the churning water below him and the moaning winds surrounding him. He sunk like a rock

Like Peter, I lost my focus during the times when things took a nosedive. I started off proudly stepping out of the boat in faith only to disappear into the murky water when I threw off Jesus' shoes of peace and replaced them with my flip-flops. I envision Jesus offering His shoes to me and I wave Him off, frustrated that the storms are coming. Did Jesus even notice the wind and the rain? The truth is, Jesus not only is aware of these storms, He knew of their existence even before they were formed. Jesus saw them coming and clearly sees through them to the slivers of light that will eventually part their darkness.

If we wear what He is offering, He will lead us through blanketed in His unending peace and not wind up the frazzled heap we usually find ourselves when the rains finally pull away. In John 14:27, Jesus tells us, "Peace I leave with you; my peace I give you. I do not give to you as the world gives. Do not let your hearts be troubled and do not be afraid."

My mom is ill. She developed a lung disease almost three years ago causing her lungs to scar, and the etiology remains a mystery. The doctors originally thought she had a bout of bronchitis. She coughed for months, but the different prescribed medications weren't working because no one knew her lung tissue was scarring. Since her diagnosis, she has been on oxygen and high doses of Prednisone which affects her immune system's ability to fight off infection. She needs the medication to breathe, but it causes so many other issues.

Since learning about her lungs scarring, my mom has fought sepsis, pneumonia, blood clots in her leg and heart, a call for a crash cart, antibiotic resistant illnesses, and numerous colds and lung infections requiring her oxygen needs to rise and rise. She is running out of usable space in her lungs, and it is frightening to watch. Within this last year, my mom has been hospitalized over a dozen times.

My mom's recent visit to the hospital was serious. We weren't sure if this time she would come home. After a sixty-five day stay at the hospital in St. Louis, she again beat the odds. She arrived home by ambulance due to her unique oxygen needs. They backed the ambulance into her driveway and when they opened the doors, she saw me holding flowers and my dad anxiously awaiting her return. When the wheels of her stretcher hit the driveway, she cried. My dad walked over to his bride, held her, and sobbed. Through his tears, my dad kept apologizing to the paramedics. He told them he didn't know if she would be coming home. I forgot I was standing there holding flowers immersed in the beautiful love I was witnessing.

My mom has been home for a week, and the roller coaster ride continues. She received some bad news from her doctor. The latest CT scans showed that her lungs are getting worse, and the pneumonia may be back. My mom has been working so hard toward gaining even the smallest amount of strength to afford her some semblance of independence. This news was a blow to our hopes.

I exercised my shoes of peace a lot during this time. It was about a thirty-minute stint one way to the hospital from where I live and incorporating the visits, fear of losing my mom, worrying about my dad, working full time, and running my active girls to their activities made me practice putting on Christ's promises, so I could walk forward in His peace and presence.

I've held my mom as she cried telling me she wished that she didn't make it during this last visit in the hospital because now her quality of life is so poor. I've witnessed my mom almost suffocate as her coughing episodes plummeted her oxygen levels into the fifties. I've seen this amazingly strong woman be whittled and shaped into someone she can no longer recognize in the mirror. Her mind is sharp, her will is strong, but her body isn't cooperating.

Even though some days my heart is heavy, and my spirit is worn out, I'm walking—and continue to walk—forward because Christ's message tells me He overcame even this. Sickness and death are not the final chapters in our story. The gospel says Christ defeated death on the cross and because of this, we have little to fear.

Our storms of life will continue to come, but we are not meant to succumb to what Jesus has already defeated. The peace comes from His death annihilating sin's hold on us. We remain living in a sinful world where hurt and pain are everywhere, but we are not bound in chains to live this pain for an eternity.

Jesus knows intimately the pain and suffering we feel because He left His throne to live among us in a world painted by sin. He suffered greatly during his life here, and He understands thoroughly what it means to experience emotional, physical, and spiritual pain. He was faithful to His Father and was not changed by circumstances or turning tides. He held steadfast and true. By dying on the cross for my soul and yours, He made a way for us to be with Him above the rolling thunder and crashing lightning and in His eternal light.

If we choose to follow Him, these temporary storms will be a blip on the screen compared to our real home in the kingdom of heaven. Jesus provides the shoes of peace so even as the storms roll through, they will not crush us. He offers us a promise that allows our feet to walk through these troubling times with joy as we look toward the horizon. "May the God of hope fill you with all joy and peace as you trust in him, so that you may overflow with hope by the power of the Holy Spirit" (Rom. 15:13).

The Shoes of Peace

Our God is omnipresent. He is with each one of us all at the same time. God is comforting the wife who lost her husband in Maryland at the same time He holds the child who lost her mother in South Africa. His hand is on the shoulder of the father kneeling at the side of his sick child's bed in Ontario while holding the hand of the executive who is cleaning out his office in Manhattan. He was with me as I wrote this book, and He is with you as you read its pages. He is the God of the universe, yet He chose a fate of torture and death on a cross, so He could lovingly and gently slip your feet into the shoes of His peace which enables you to weather even the strongest of cyclones. He is our Savior. We aren't meant to perish in these storms but to learn dependence on His abilities to see us through. We are meant to be His.

During our children's trying moments, we hug them, comfort them, love them, and will our peace onto them, so they feel a sense of strength and stability during their trials. Our Father will not leave us in the same way we will not leave our own children, but—like our own children—we are given the will to decide to either fall into our Father's arms or turn our backs on Him and try to forge ahead on our own. I've done the latter so many times that now my first instinct is no longer to run away but to be enveloped in my Father's embrace. My scars remind me of the battles I have fought alone. I choose the shoes of peace because I experienced their amazing ability to keep me moving forward. I carry so many unnecessary scars. I pray you can experience His peace faster than I was willing to because His promises are true. Turn to Him and find out for yourself.

The beautiful part about the shoes of peace is what they are constructed from—the good news of Jesus Christ! They aren't assembled from any earthly material that will rot or decay. The shoes are crafted with the impenetrable truth of the dying and raising of our Lord and Savior! They will never wear out, the straps will never break, we will never outgrow them, and they will never fail us.

We can be like that heroic man drowning out all that is crashing down around us and focusing only on the voice of our Savior telling us, "I've got this!" Those lies, addictions, worries, and mountains in our lives become rubble under our feet and because of this, we are now able to move! Shoes are intended to help us put one foot in front of the other in a forward motion. We have places to go with Christ's shoes on. I can picture with each step we take the rocks are turning into dust under our feet, and rays of light are shooting out from our toes to illuminate the path God wants us to take.

Sometimes our path takes us down some narrow alleyways or through some difficult terrain, but the purpose of the shoes is not to avoid life's landmines but to get through them unharmed. Don't we grow so much more during the trials we survive compared to the moments we coast through? When we walk through the tough terrain and survive, we can better help others who are entering the same unfortunate path we now have in our rearview mirror. We can point them to the author of peace and let them rest on the warm and sunny rock of all creation.

Like buying and wearing a pair of shoes to make a fashion statement, wearing the shoes of peace are an advertisement in their own right. Have you ever looked at a person walking through so much turmoil with grace and hope and wonder, "How are they doing that?"

Walking in peace while going through the dark times provides an opportunity for the good news to be shared. Metaphorically, they are looking at our shoes and asking themselves, "What shoes are they wearing, so they are able to keep walking forward?" We

The Shoes of Peace

can confidently answer them, "Jesus is the author of the peace I have. Hold my hand, and I'll show you what I mean." Could we walk along with someone else while going through life's dips and turns without the shoes of peace? It would be difficult to do.

As we move through these battles, the sole focus isn't for our own self-preservation. It is so we can confidently move forward sharing the gospel and have an answer for why we are so at peace. This doesn't mean we aren't allowed to honor our feelings of sorrow, fear, anger, worry, or pain. It means we are not living a life without hope. We have a Savior who wants us to look forward—toward Him—as the ground under us rolls.

Jesus wasn't offered an easy life while He was here. He lived with great difficulty, but through the strength of His Father, Jesus continued preaching and serving. Even though Jesus felt pain, anger, and sorrow just like us, He extended His hands to others and guided them towards the conclusion we are all meant to have—an eternal relationship with Him. Once our footing is sure, we can then shine a light on the shoes Christ furnished, so others can learn of the peace and joy they provide.

By wearing the belt of truth, we are avoiding the many landmines placed in our life by the enemy. By wearing the breastplate of righteousness, our cleansed hearts are free to hear the words of our Savior, so we can act according to His will. By wearing the shoes of peace, no matter what chaos surrounds us, we can look straight ahead and continue the path God planned for each one of us. Let's pray the shoes of peace into our lives to add to God's armor, so we can defy the weapons of our enemy.

"Dear heavenly Father, I want to trade in the shoes I've been wearing for way too long for the ones made by Christ. I want to walk in His peace and comfort as I try to move forward against the wind and rain that always seem to come. I don't want to huddle or hide anymore from my circumstances but want hope despite them. I want to live the life you intended for me, and I am ready to give all my burdens, fears, and worries to you and leave them at the foot of the cross. I trust in your message of hope, peace, and life and ask you to slip these beautiful shoes onto my feet, so I can walk with the assured steps you originally intended for me. In your precious name I pray. Amen."

THE SHIELD OF FAITH

In addition to all this, take up the shield of faith, with which you can extinguish all the flaming arrows of the evil one. (Eph. 6:16)

CHAPTER 5
―――――――

TO SHIELD OR NOT TO SHIELD?

As I am writing this, it is raining outside. Rain has a way of lulling us into hibernation-mode, catapulting reading and napping to the forefront of our desires. After we wrestle and lose the struggle because the demands of our day are calling, we reluctantly yank off the covers and leave the comfort of our beds. Knowing we are confronting the wetness and cold outside of our warm homes, we at least can take solace in the fact we have a trusty umbrella to make our venture outside a little easier.

We put a lot of faith in this small device, depending on its metal handle and vinyl canopy to shield us from those pesky drops. It affords us the ability to step out into the rain and walk across a parking lot toward our places of work, store, or a daycare drop-off. The umbrella works perfectly until the wind picks up, and the rain blows sideways. Our drenched pants let us know our shield suddenly lost its effectiveness.

What is the role of a shield? For a Roman soldier, the shield was designed to stop the onslaught of weapons attempting to end their advancement forward. Sometimes, the Romans would gather and use their shields as a unified wall. By working together, they could shield themselves from much greater threats than if they acted alone.

We rely on lots of things in our lives to shield our own advancements forward. Our hands shield our eyes when we are the unlucky person positioned in a conversation facing the sun. Our houses shield us from the weather, and our coats shield us from the cold. If you think about it, we spend a good part of our time shielding ourselves, or paying for things that shield us, from one circumstance or another.

On a scorcher of a day, our backyard trees provide shade from the beating sun creating a moment of coolness when mowing the lawn. I'm constantly worried about my husband when he works outside. I remind him to slather suntan lotion on his head and wear a hat to protect him from an unwanted sunburn or worse.

Children who are afraid of a storm use their parent's body to shield them from the scary sounds. Were you the one who went into a haunted house and situated yourself behind a friend and transformed them into your human shield as they were forced to be the first ones to walk the dark passageway and enter the creepy room?

Physical shields are necessary, but so are the emotional shields we try to create to protect our children from the things of this broken world. We attempt to shield and protect our kids from the *what ifs* of life, and we hope we guessed correctly which shields are needed and which ones aren't important. We give them information about drugs, advice about friendships, and cautionary tales from our own painful experiences as we try to impart the wisdom we learned along the way. When we don't foresee the one thing that got through our defenses, we kick ourselves and wonder how we didn't see that coming.

We don't have the powerful omniscience to see every curve ball heading toward us, but we are fortunate enough to have a God who

The Shield of Faith

does. He knows when the winds will shift, and the rain will blow sideways. When we depend upon our own shields, we realize too late we relied on the wrong shield and feel the consequences of its limited and ineffective protection.

When my oldest daughter was five, we went to a local pizza shop to pick up a pizza we ordered for dinner. When we left the store, she was walking next to me while I carried the large pizza and drinks. It was a small parking lot, and we were the only car. As I kept walking toward our car, she paused to walk along the parking blocks by the front door of the store with her pink bear in the crook of her arm. I hadn't noticed her detour until I heard her cry. When she was balancing on the blocks, she miss-stepped and fell scraping her legs and hand.

In her memory—and how she retells this story—she fell because I didn't hold her hand as she walked along the concrete block. In her eyes, it was my fault I didn't notice she stopped to play, and I willfully missed the opportunity to prevent her fall from happening. I failed to see far enough into the future to take every precaution to ensure her safety. I think this caused her more hurt than the actual fall. Our previous talks of staying close to mommy and to not walk on those blocks didn't factor into her thinking. She was upset my usually reliable shield of protection fell short, and it made her feel insecure in my abilities.

In our daily lives it can also feel like our own personal shields are falling short. On some days more than others, mud and rocks can sling at us faster than we can move out of the way. A missed alarm in the morning can snowball into being late for a meeting while you are stuck in traffic with spilled coffee on your lap. When you get to work, the school nurse calls, and your child is sick. At home, the fridge is empty, and payday is a week away. In my house when one appliance stops working, I can pretty much guarantee on the horizon two or three other things will be falling apart as well. It seems life is forever slinging things at us making any forward advancement feel like we are walking against the wind.

Sometimes life slings more than daily irritations and disappointments. We have moments where we are facing the loss of a loved one or the worry and fear of losing someone who is ill. We battle through financial strains, job losses, breakups, and breakdowns which are a small part of the litany of life's struggles we can write on a scroll that rolls on for miles and miles.

It's a proven fact we can't create a shield that protects us from these sufferings. Some of us try to white-knuckle the reins of our lives wanting to believe so badly we are the ones in control. That is until the rug is pulled out from under us, and our problems bucked us off the saddle. We may find ourselves questioning, "How could this have happened?" Sometimes we turn our attention to God and ask Him, "Why didn't you save me from this?" or "Why didn't you hold my hand as I walked on top of the parking lot blocks and stop this painful event from occurring?" We may even assume God willfully chose to not be close by because we're now engulfed in the flames of a bad situation with nowhere to turn. Why didn't He protect us?

Just as the shoes of peace keep us moving forward despite all we must walk over, our faith shield is designed to block the arrows, so we can advance forward—but that doesn't mean the arrows will stop coming. They will always come while we live in a world occupied by Satan. When we choose in the morning to not pick up our shield but instead brace ourselves from the sting of the flaming arrows on our own, we are choosing in that moment to put our faith in ourselves and not in Christ. When the flames hit and burn, we question God's abilities and forget about all the previous warnings He has given to us about Satan's attacks. Did we proactively position the shield in front of us when the arrows started to fall? Did we reach out for His extended hand before we miss-stepped?

I can readily admit to the many times I was caught without my shield as I ignored God's hand and ran in the wrong direction. The arrows in my life had no shield to stop them, and their capabilities were at full strength when they hit their target. I put my faith in myself and decided I could control the situation. My faith should have been in God, my Father, who loves me. I left my faith in Him at the door, walked around His shield of protection, and stepped over the threshold into the attacks that were waiting.

In Galatians 3:26, Paul tells us, "So in Christ Jesus you are all children of God through faith." We are His children, and He wants to properly shield us, but we have some responsibility in this as well. We can't carry two shields—His and ours. We must be willing to put down our own shields and give Him our full faith and trust.

What is God's shield able to accomplish that ours can't? His shield is the only one that disarms the flaming arrows, so their toxins are neutralized. We can keep advancing forward even when everything around us seems impossible. The winds can blow in any direction, and God's shield will be enough; it will never be ineffective. "But he said to me, 'My grace is sufficient for you, for my power is made perfect in weakness.' Therefore I will boast all the more gladly about my weaknesses, so that Christ's power may rest on me" (2 Cor. 12:9).

My youngest daughter carries a confidence shield that is strong and mighty. She lets little deter her and sometimes as her parent, my own darts of doubt about her latest ideas don't seem to ever hit their target. When she was in the third grade, she decided she was going to enter the third-grade talent show and planned on whistling the "Star-Spangled Banner." My fears of her not doing well or that it wasn't a good enough talent didn't stop her from the pursuit of this idea. She practiced and practiced in her bedroom and the day of the talent show, I was white knuckling my chair. Not only did she do fantastic, she ignored the loud, clanging disruption that came when pots were accidentally dropped in the school's kitchen which was nearby. My daughter didn't miss a beat; she kept on whistling.

She was born with this shield of confidence, and it is something I always admired. God's shield works in this same way. No matter what arrows fly in our direction, our forward motion will not be halted. Our confidence comes from knowing God is the shield we carry, and we shouldn't let the clanging disruptions of our lives stop us from pursuing His will.

If life's hurts get to a point we can no longer hold up our own shield, we should ask those with faith to encircle us like the Roman soldiers and create a wall until our strength is restored. Our Father didn't leave us without protection. He gave us His Son, and He gave us each other:

> Two are better than one, because they have a good return for their labor: If either of them falls down, one can help the other up. But pity anyone who falls and has no one to help them up. Also, if two lie down together, they will keep warm. But how can one keep warm alone? Though one may be overpowered, two can defend themselves. A cord of three strands is not quickly broken. (Eccles. 4:19–12)

When we put our faith in Christ, we gain the ability to look up and focus on His strength and away from the darkness trying to distract us with its fear. He will protect us, love us, and keep us even when the impossible is occurring. Jesus already conquered the

The Shield of Faith

impossible, so our faith needs to be with Him who is unconquerable. When we learn to trust and allow our faith shield to grow in strength, we can look at the flaming arrows heading toward us without despair. Christ already took our pain, hurt, fears, and inequities with Him to the cross, and He is more than strong enough to shield us from anything the enemy tries to throw.

Christ has proven time and again in my own life that His promises are true, and what I labeled impossible, He renamed defeated. Satan knows he only has a short time to reign because the Bible tells us Jesus will create a new heaven and a new earth, and Satan will be tossed into the lake of fire. His days are numbered, and he wants to take as many of us with him as he is able.

For him to succeed, he needs us to leave our shields by the front door. He is fully aware he is no match for Jesus, and he is taking advantage of his reign by working overtime to find those who are unprotected. Have you checked out the recent news stories? I'd say with each passing day we are becoming more and more of a society not willing to carry the right shield of protection. The winds are blowing, and we are getting awfully wet.

If you give into the thought that Satan isn't seeking you—whether to keep you from taking up the shield of faith or to trick you into putting it down—remember even Jesus was relentlessly tempted during His forty days in the desert. Jesus never succumbed to Satan's appealing temptations, but that didn't stop Satan from trying again and again. He wouldn't leave Jesus alone. When the forty days of fasting ended, Jesus remained sinless and never gave into the temptations Satan offered. Even so, Satan still wouldn't admit defeat. He refused to roll up his temptation tackle box and end his pursuit of Jesus. Satan is a patient opportunist and after trying and failing to tempt Jesus, he simply decided he would try again later.

If Satan refused to give up tempting the Savior of the world and God's Holy Son, why in the world would he give up on us whom God loves, and he hates? He won't. Those fiery darts of temptation, fear, hurt, pain, disappointment, worry, angst, concern, sadness, despair, job loss, money problems, broken hearts, and feeling overwhelmed will not cease because we carry God's shield. They will always keep coming as long as Satan is still freely about this world.

With our shield of faith, we can stop those darts from turning into their true purpose: freezing our advancement forward. He wants us to quit actively pursuing God's plan for our lives by tucking us into the shadows of our own sorrow-filled caves. We can't be light and salt of this world if we are broken, defeated, and faithless. "I have been crucified with Christ and I no longer live, but Christ lives in me. The life I now live in the body, I live by faith in the Son of God, who loved me and gave himself for me" (Gal. 2:20).

Satan's arsenal is extensive, and he would love for us to remain unguarded. A scenario of someone not shielding themselves properly may look and sound something like this:

DART NUMBER ONE IS FIRED:

Satan whispers: "You are so much better than him."

Ed: "I can't believe he got that promotion over me. I am much more qualified than him. This place is ridiculous. I'm tired of being looked over, and if they don't watch out, I may quit!"

Satan: "Dart number one was a dead hit."

DART NUMBER TWO IS FIRED:

Satan: "Your wife doesn't respect you like Jana does."

Ed: "Look at my wife happily talking to the neighbors. She is much nicer to them than she ever is to me. All I get is complaints and nagging. My secretary, Jana, is the only one that pays any attention to me. I should ask her out to dinner one night to show her my appreciation."

Satan: "Dart number two hit the bullseye."

DART NUMBER THREE IS FIRED:

Satan: "You work hard. You deserve to treat yourself."

Ed: "Why does John always have a nicer car than me? He doesn't work nearly as hard as I do. I deserve to be treated. That's it. I'm going tomorrow to trade in this family-mobile. Barbara will have to deal with it. I make the money in this house, not her!"

Satan: "Lock and load, boys. Dart number three was a success. We got him where we want him."

DART NUMBER FOUR IS FIRED:

Satan: "This is purely innocent. Barbara doesn't need to know."

Ed: "Jana said yes! Finally, I have something to look forward to. I'll let Barb know I have a dinner meeting. It won't take long. It's only a quick bite out."

Satan: "Perfect hit. Dart number four split the heart."

DART NUMBER FIVE IS FIRED:

Satan: "How dare they question you?"

Ed: "Barbara is such a pill! And that crazy friend of hers saying I was out cheating on her. It was just dinner with my secretary! It's no big deal. If I wanted to hide it, I wouldn't have eaten at a place where someone may see me. I'm going to text Jana. I need to unload this on someone, and she is such a great listener."

Satan: "Dart number five hit right between the eyes. That's a wrap for now, boys. Ed's got it from here."

Here is that same scenario if Ed was using his shield and placing his faith and trust in the only One who can protect us from Satan's quest to seek, kill, and destroy.

DART NUMBER ONE IS FIRED:

Satan: "You are so much better than him."

Ed: "Well, I prayed I would get that promotion, but for some reason it wasn't God's will for my life or my family's life right now. Even though it hurts, I have faith He has something better for me on the horizon. I can't possibly know what the future holds, but I am so glad my God knows intimately what my needs are. I need to go over to Paul and congratulate him."

Satan: "Dart number one was a miss. We will try another tactic."

DART NUMBER TWO IS FIRED:

Satan: "She is nicer to the neighbors than she is to you."

Ed: "Barbara and I have been drifting lately. This isn't God's best for us. He wants us to be partners—not roommates. The enemy loves to destroy marriages. Please, Lord, protect mine. We've been so busy with the kids and work, and it doesn't seem like we have spent any time together or even talked much lately. I don't feel like talking to the neighbors right now, but I will go over there and try to be social. That would make Barb smile since she is the social one in the neighborhood, not me. Then I will suggest we grab dinner out tonight—just the two of us. We need to stop this drift before it gets worse."

The Shield of Faith

Satan: "That didn't work, either. His faith is strong. We'll have to work harder to get around this shield."

DART NUMBER THREE IS FIRED:

Satan: "You always provide for your family. You deserve to treat yourself."

Ed: "The debt feels like it's piling up. Michael's medical bills are now rolling in from breaking his arm, Barb's car is on the fritz, and her hours got cut. Lord, I don't know how we will make it, but I have faith you will provide; you always do. I need to put my worries into your hands and trust you will make a way. Please shield us from these financial storms. They are out of my control, but I know nothing is too big for you, Lord. Help us and guide us through this tough time."

Satan: "This isn't getting through. We need to ratchet up the temptation."

DART NUMBER FOUR IS FIRED:

Satan: "I think she likes you."

Ed: "Barb always tells me I am no good with subtleties, and I need to be hit over the head to notice something, but I think Jana is trying to flirt with me. I'm not sure, but I need to pray about this and ask God to reveal to me the truth and give me the courage to stop this before it gets out of hand. I have faith my God will protect me from this temptation and give me the right words to put a stop to it. Lord, shield my marriage and my job from anything the enemy is trying to destroy."

Satan: "We need to re-strategize. There will be a time when his shield is down, and we will hit our target. We must watch and wait. Let's hold things back for a while. We want him to feel comfortable, so he lets his defenses down."

In this example, which Ed would you want to be? Can you think of a time when you were head nodding to the whispers about all you deserved and all you had a right to, even if it meant hurting someone you loved? The outcome of these situations never meets our expectations, and we wind up worse than when we started. We wish in these moments we could turn back time and shield ourselves appropriately.

The Bible is chock-full of examples where people used their shield of faith, those who didn't, and what their perspective outcomes were. Noah had faith enough to build an Arc on land far removed from water despite everyone he knew questioning and mocking him. Even though they ignored his warnings, he continued God's chosen assignment for him. It wasn't of consequence to Noah that other people didn't understand his purpose or ridiculed the Arc he was building. The only thing that mattered was Noah's faith rested in God's plan—not man's plan.

Daniel was thrown into the lion's den because King Darius was tricked into signing a decree that stated anyone worshiping someone other than the king will perish in this way. The fiery dart of jealousy hit other men in King Darius' administration, and these men decided to trap Daniel—a known worshiper of God. They were jealous of the king's trust in Daniel and wanted to destroy him. Daniel was in an impossible situation and even though the king learned too late of the trap's intention, King Darius reluctantly had no choice but to sentence Daniel to face the lions.

Daniel's shield of faith was a fortress around him and protected him from feelings of fear or despair. Daniel could still advance forward without faltering and because of his faith, God rescued him from the lion's jaws. King Darius was amazed and ordered his whole kingdom to worship our one true God. Because of Daniel's faith, he single-handedly altered the object of worship from a human king to our heavenly King.

THE SHIELD OF FAITH

Before Daniel was sentenced to the lion's den, Satan used the same fiery dart of jealousy to send Shadrach, Meshach, and Abednego—Daniel's friends—into a burning furnace. Their strong faith in God allowed them to confidently tell King Nebuchadnezzar if it was God's will to save them, He would, and if not, they were willing to serve God unto death. Either way, they believed in the greater plan of God. God chose to rescue them from the fire and because of their faith, King Nebuchadnezzar protected the right to worship our God and punished anyone who spoke out against Him.

As a young boy, David was chosen by God to be the destined king of Israel. The problem was, he didn't look the part. David was comparably smaller and less impressive than his older brothers who were fighting on the front lines while David attended sheep, yet God chose him to be king. It was laughable to those around him that God would choose this puny kid to reign over Israel and decided God's plan surely must be faulty. It didn't make much sense to anyone.

Human eyes fail to see the condition of the human heart, and God doesn't rely on our human measuring stick to determine someone's worth. He knew David's faith was strong, and that is what made him worthy. Because David's faith was in God's strength—not his own strength—he had the courage to volunteer and fight Goliath even as the greatest soldiers around him cowered, including his brothers.

God didn't provide the soldier's arsenal to defend David—which was ill-fitting and awkward—but used the smallest of weapons, a slingshot, to win against the impossible. God can use anything to bring down the giants in our own lives if we have faith.

David wasn't made a king right away but had to wait many years. How often do we say the same thing about what we want to happen in our own lives? We don't trust in God's plan, or He is taking too long to answer our prayers, so we try to circumvent His ways because we know better. We throw down our shields losing faith in God's perfect timing.

The Bible also gives examples of people who lost their faith. The Israelites wandered the desert for forty years because they feared the giants in the Promised Land. They missed out on God's best for them because they succumbed to their fear and lost all their faith. Didn't God part the Red Sea for them to escape Egypt? You would think they had more reason than anyone to have faith that God could defeat the current inhabitants of Israel. Because they had no faith, they missed out on the land of milk and honey and wandered until that generation of people died.

When the people of Israel wanted a king like a king in other nations, God acquiesced to their demands. God can't force people to have faith in His plans. Israel chose their first king based on worldly measures and much discord followed. Again, how often do we lay down our shields of protection and go after the one thing God does not want us to have?

God promised Abraham and Sarah a baby and feeling like God's plan was taking too long, Abraham had a baby with another woman. Anger and strife ensued between these two families, and we still feel the effects of this division today. When we force God's plan to move faster, we only wind up feeling the lasting results of its consequences. "He replied, 'Because you have so little faith. Truly I tell you, if you have faith as small as a mustard seed, you can say to this mountain, "Move from here to there," and it will move. Nothing will be impossible for you'" (Matt. 17:20).

Carrying God's shield of faith isn't initially an easy thing to do. The Roman shield is heavy. It takes great strength and practice to learn to hold up that type of shield, and the same is true for our

The Shield of Faith

shield of faith. The ease of holding our shield comes from exercising our faith during those times of adversity. I don't know how many times I had to fall flat to realize I'm not adequately protecting myself from Satan's arrows. The shield felt too cumbersome, the time was taking too long, the plan seemed flawed, and God didn't seem to know what He was doing, so I laid down the shield to take care of my own business. If this sounds familiar to you, then you too experienced the fallout that can occur.

If a Roman soldier laid down their shield in battle because they never gained the strength to hold it, they most likely wouldn't make it three feet before they were killed. My shield is light as a feather now. I've grown in my faith and continue to grow each day because through practice, I've learned to lift my shield during difficult times instead of laying it down. Every time I lifted my faith shield, Jesus showed me by putting my faith and trust in Him, I would not falter. "If any of you lacks wisdom, you should ask God, who gives generously to all without finding fault, and it will be given to you. But when you ask, you must believe and not doubt, because the one who doubts is like a wave of the sea, blown and tossed by the wind" (James 1:5–6). Don't be blown by the winds that are sure to come but carry your shield of faith confidently. It's waiting for you by the front door.

Let's pray the shield of faith into our lives and embrace the protection that God provides. We are in a war, and we need to be shielded from Satan's schemes with the only shield that can truly protect us—our Faith.

"Dear heavenly Father, even though we gave up Eden where shields were not necessary, and we could walk freely with you in the Garden, you gave us protection in this flawed world from the same schemes the devil used to tempt Adam and Eve. Your ways are not cumbersome, and your shield is light for all who have faith.

Please surround me with your arms of protection and keep my faith in you held firmly out in front of me as I walk forward on the path you are asking me to take. Let my shield extinguish every dart of temptation because I know you are always with me. I hold up my shield because you know the past, present, and future happenings of my life, and you are all powerful. I willingly put my faith and trust in the one true God and His Holy Son, and I can't wait for the day where the shield of protection is no longer needed because we are freely able to walk with you again. I pray this in Jesus' Holy name. Amen."

HELMET OF SALVATION

Take the helmet of salvation. (Eph. 6:17)

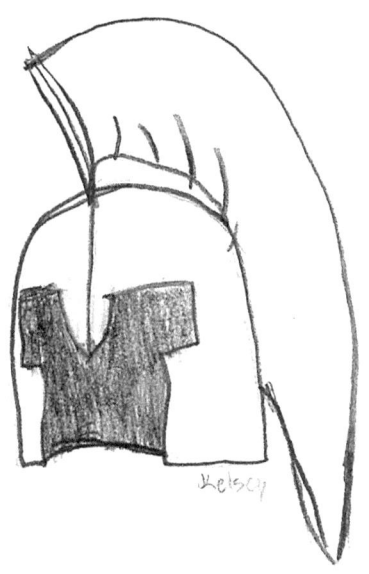

Chapter 6

ALWAYS WEAR YOUR HELMET!

When I was a kid in the seventies and eighties, I didn't know anyone who wore a helmet unless they were riding a motorcycle. We had a lot less safety precautions in place back then, and helmet wearing wasn't even on the radar. What damage could a little bike ride do if you didn't wear a helmet on your head and you kissed concrete–unfortunately a lot. Did they even sell bike helmets thirty or forty years ago for kids?

My brother is three years older than I am and when I was in elementary school, he built a bike from different parts he had gathered from older bikes. The pedals were a little long for the body of the bike, and he warned me to be careful and keep the pedals horizontal when I turned so they didn't scrape the ground.

Well, as his kid sister, I didn't listen to his warning and took off down the street on his bike. I made a sharp turn, and the pedal became an instant emergency brake as it connected with the road; it halted the bike but not my progression forward. I flipped headfirst over the handlebars. God was watching out for me, though. As I was laying there on the street flat on my back crying, a neighbor came out and called for my brother and his friends to come and help me. I was cut and scraped from my shoulders to my shins, but my head wasn't hurt. It could have been a lot worse.

Today, an abundance of money is spent on designing and testing helmets to ensure their quality and durability will stand up against an impact. Design production and testing is included for military helmets, bike helmets, motorcycle helmets, skateboarding and equestrian riding helmets, skiing helmets, jockey helmets, race car driver helmets, football helmets, baseball helmets, and the list goes on.

Roman soldiers relied heavily on their helmets. In a physical battle, what use would their other armor be without a helmet? Leaving their heads exposed and vulnerable makes it almost silly to wear any of the other battle gear. Without their heads, the rest of their body wouldn't function for long. A Roman soldier without his helmet would be picked off one by one like plucking the fluffy seeds from a dandelion.

As good as our current technology is at improving our safety when wearing a helmet, there is a helmet much stronger than anything we could ever create with our own hands. When David stepped up and said he'd challenge Goliath, he was offered—but refused—the helmet made of bronze. He tried it on, but it didn't feel right to him. The physical protection offered wasn't fitting correctly. Even though he was facing a giant who was covered in armor from head to toe, David didn't see the need to match his adversary gear for gear. His helmet was of far greater value and offered substantially more protection than the one he was presented with, or the one the giant had donned. David was guarded with the helmet of salvation, and we all know who the victor was in this battle.

We are given the choice to wear whatever helmet we please as we go along our life's journey, but when it's the wrong type of helmet, it causes more headaches and pain than protection. A

The Helmet of Salvation

football helmet is excellent protection during a football game, but I wouldn't wear a football helmet while riding a horse. Not seeing while riding atop of a galloping, one-thousand-pound animal—as my helmet bounced and shifted on my undersized head—would almost guarantee a disaster than prevent one. My wrong helmet choice could cause irreparable damage.

If we are choosing to rely on saving ourselves or others saving us, it would be like wearing that football helmet and riding an untamed Stallion. David sized up the helmet offered by Saul and decided he didn't need a helmet made of bronze–he needed a helmet made of God. David decided against man's helmet, took the helmet of salvation, and defeated the supposedly undefeatable.

The one thing I love about this piece of armor is the first word Paul uses when introducing the helmet of salvation. Paul didn't say Jesus would place the helmet of salvation on our head. He said, *Take*. Just as in the shield of faith, we are asked to take this piece of armor into our hands. A physical act on our part is necessary to take something. Our arms must be held out in front of us, palms facing each other, and fingers ready to grab ahold of the helmet. We need to willfully accept its purpose as we lift it and position it on our heads.

Let's look at the word *take* for a minute. I use this word all the time but now that I am zeroing in on it to analyze, I see many layers I never thought of before. It's a pretty strong word if you think about it. If someone takes something from you, it's an intentional, conscious decision on their part. They didn't accidentally *take* your wallet, or it didn't happen to flip out of your pocket and into their unsuspecting hands. It was a planned and executed action with the sole purpose of making your pocket a little lighter.

If I *take* my kids to one of their activities, there is a whole behind-the-scenes frenzy happening for me to get them from point

A to point B. It usually involves running around the house trying to find something fast to put in their bellies, making sure homework is done to avoid the ten o'clock, cross-eyed experience of finding the elusive answer to social studies question number thirty-eight, and other obligations are shifted and arrangements are made if one kid needs to be picked up at the same time the other kid needs delivery to their activity. Sound familiar? If someone asks me what I am doing that evening and I say, "I have to take my daughters to band practice and soccer," there is a lot more involved than that simple statement implies.

The same is true when Paul says, "Take the helmet of salvation." He doesn't mean grab it from a pile of helmets rusting in the corner of a shed. There is only one helmet Paul is referring to, and for us to willfully and consciously take it, a lot must happen behind the scenes. To take and wear the helmet of salvation, you must accept the gift by which it was created. The helmet isn't made of any material that could break down from the elements of this world. It's made of an everlasting material that Christ has given to us. Without Christ, we have no helmet.

How do we take the helmet of salvation? What does salvation even mean? Salvation is being saved from the sin punishment we all deserve and receiving what we don't deserve—living freely in Christ Jesus who is the only one with the power to write our names in the Lamb's Book of Life. When we are ready to acknowledge our need of a savior, we accept Jesus' sacrificial death on the cross as He painfully took our sins with Him. We believe Jesus saves us by His blood that now washes us clean. We repent of, which means to turn away from, our sins and ask for forgiveness from Christ who has the authority to forgive. If we do these things, the helmet of salvation is made available to each one of us. By humbling ourselves

The Helmet of Salvation

before the Lord and asking Him to save us from our sin punishment, we are saved from what we truly deserve: an eternal separation from Him.

Can you imagine if God gave us what we legitimately deserved on this side of heaven? With a switch of the TV channels we are painfully made aware of the horrible acts committed almost daily around our planet. I often wonder why God doesn't zap us all and say, "I've had it. I can't take this anymore!" We break His heart every single second of every day. God isn't only privy to the sad and desperate things we see on the news. He witnesses every painful suffering and evil thing that takes place that we don't see because He is omnipresent. God endures an unimaginable broken heart.

He intimately knows what our sin does to each other and suffers this horrific pain because in His great love for us, He yearns for as many souls as possible to take the helmet of salvation offered by His precious Son. There will be a day when Christ will come and wipe away sin from this planet for an eternity, and our time to decide will end. Until then, God will continue to see what we do to ourselves and each other even when we believe no one is watching. He is watching, and He is constantly saddened by the results of the fall.

When we do witness or experience the sad things, the sadness doesn't last forever. Our painful seasons of life cycle through and are replaced with moments of peace, love, and happiness. God never gets a break from what He sees. Remember, this isn't the world that He had in mind for us. This is the world that we chose, and He constantly must behold the fallout.

As sin and evil run rampant, He continues to blanket us with blue skies and gorgeous sunsets, budding flowers and changing leaves, chirping birds and grandbaby kisses, cool breezes and ocean waves. God is the author and creator of everything good, and these are all reflections of who God is. His love for us is shown through His creativity and affords us the ability to experience these gifts every day whether we choose to accept His gift of salvation or not. He extends these magnificent daily reminders letting us know He is still here with us as He patiently waits for us to acknowledge His presence.

If we choose to not take the helmet of salvation and ignore His offer, we are solidifying our choice to not be in communion with Him. God will, with a heavy heart, accept our choice and give us what we asked for—an eternity that is separated from Him. When you pass away, picture all the beauty, love, and good things of this world being instantaneously erased, and what's left is what you chose.

We know all too well we can't force people to love us because our will allows us to choose. When we choose not to love someone, we choose not to have a relationship with them. When they do leave, they take with them the core of who they are that at one time colored our world. The same is true with God. It's a relationship with you that He seeks, but if He forced you into a relationship with Him, is that true love and friendship or a relationship manufactured out of fear? That is the tactic Satan uses, not God. He will honor what you did choose and give you a life apart from Him. The core of all that God is—love, beauty, honor—will be gone forever.

Salvation can't be earned. The Bible doesn't tell us if we only prayed more, attended church, helped the poor, and became a better person, God would then love us. Doing these things is the equivalent of us hammering our own helmet made of bronze and saying, "Look God, isn't it pretty?" We don't do these things to earn our salvation; we do these things because of our salvation.

When you have a relationship with your spouse or friends, you do things to foster that relationship. You don't eat dinner with them, send a birthday card, or make a phone call to earn a friend or spouse. You do these things because you are trying to show your love and appreciation for the relationship you already have with them. You do these things to stay connected. What we do for God isn't so He can fill in a grade on our report card. When we are in a relationship with God, we do these things, so we can stay connected to Him.

If you believe attending church and reading your Bible will save you, or if you think salvation is way out of your grasp because of all the things you failed to do in your life, you are listening to the lie of the one who is selling football helmets at an amazingly low price. Truthfully, it's the highest price you could ever pay for something so wrong.

If you've backed yourself into a dark corner of the world thinking you placed yourself too far for Jesus to reach you, remember who created the world. There isn't a place you can hide that He does not see. He can see as clearly in the dark as He can in the light. He is standing with you in that dark place, loving you, and offering you His hand to guide you into the sun to melt away the bone-chilling cold that is trying to cover you.

Satan also spreads the false idea that the helmet of salvation is cumbersome, uncomfortable, and holds us back. He sells the lie that salvation is awkward, it doesn't allow us to have any fun, and others will think we are nuts for wearing it. If that doesn't work, he spins it so we believe that salvation is difficult to acquire, and we must jump through all sorts of hoops even to be worthy of such a helmet. The truth is our salvation through Jesus Christ is liberating and freeing. The Holy Spirit floods into our bodies and we grow in wisdom and discernment identifying the shadows from the light: the lies from the truth. We will continue to have burdens this side of heaven, but He will make our burdens weightless and carry even the heaviest of loads for us.

Our freedom comes from avoiding the wrong paths as we hear the voice of our Lord telling us which way to turn and which bait is meant to harm us. Our enjoyment comes from not living a life of regret and sorrow but living a life to its fullest despite the trials that will come. Our joy is no longer situational. It comes from our knowledge that these trials will not last forever. Our salvation not only sets us free in this world but offers us our freedom from the clutches of the evil one and his house of pain for an eternity. We get to celebrate in the house of the Lord and live without fear, without sorrow, and without pain for all the days to come. We get to live with our God—and our King—as He always intended.

When we become a child of God, the definition of who we are is redefined, and all our past regrets, sufferings, painful childhoods, and poor choices no longer have a hold on us. We are set free. Satan wants you to believe that football helmets are perfect for horseback riding. It's your choice to believe him or not.

Another amazing thing about our God is there isn't a time limit. Some people accept Jesus' gift on the cross at a young age. Some people, like me, accept it when they are middle-aged. There are also some people who will accept it on their deathbed and any time in between. We are not made more righteous the younger we believe, but we receive the benefit of living the blessings of a righteous life longer through Christ Jesus. I know I wish I was living His righteous life when I was younger. I would have avoided many more agonizing experiences formed by taking all the wrong paths because I had chosen to wear the wrong helmet on my head.

When Jesus was nailed to the cross, there were two criminals hanging on their own crosses. Both criminals deserved to be there. One of the criminals acknowledged he deserved his fate and recognized Jesus did nothing to deserve to be crucified. The other criminal scoffed at them both and held on to his hardened heart.

The Helmet of Salvation

The criminal that admitted his crimes asked Jesus to bring him into heaven. He accepted his need for Jesus during his last moments of life. Jesus didn't respond with, "Well, it's a little too late for that, buddy! Where were you when I was performing miracles and preaching the Bible? Plus, you haven't read enough Bible verses, attended enough church services, or performed enough acts of kindness to deserve forgiveness." Instead, even while bearing the torture on the cross so sins can be forgiven that still reaches clear into my time and yours, He gently answered this man with, "Truly I tell you, today you will be with me in paradise" (Luke 23:43).

While writing these chapters, this one has brought me to tears. Feeling the enormity of the weight of my sins—and the undeserving helmet that I can freely take and put on my head—is almost too much. As things go well, we easily take for granted the seriousness of what our sinful natures did to Jesus. As His limbs were being hammered to wood and He was hoisted into the air to suffocate and die a criminal's death, His sentence wasn't for one crime, it was for the crimes of every sin that has ever been committed. Every. Single. Sin. That is a lifetime of one person's sins multiplied by the multitudes of people who have lived, are living, and will live on Earth. It is a number that is unfathomable. It's a staggering list of charges Jesus accepted on the cross that will continue to grow throughout the generations until He comes again.

A sinless man bore an impossible conviction, and the sins I committed yesterday, today, and will commit tomorrow are what put Him there. It's an overwhelming and incredibly humbling feeling to know Jesus did this for me, and He did this for you. Jesus didn't pick and choose who He did this for because He did this for all who are willing to accept the selfless gift of His death, so we don't have to take His place.

His raising to life meant our sins can't own us if we repent of them and keep them on the cross where they belong. It's too much for us to carry, and there is nothing we can do to wash ourselves clean. That is why Jesus willingly did this for us. The sin of Adam and Eve sentenced us to a life of pain, suffering, and death, but the life, death, and resurrection of Jesus saves all of humanity from this becoming our eternal penalty. "For just as through the disobedience of the one man the many were made sinners, so also through the obedience of the one man the many will be made righteous" (Rom. 5:19).

If God is so loving and kind, why doesn't He automatically save all of us? I mean, if He doesn't want anyone to perish, why aren't we all given a free ticket into heaven? The reason is simple. God is perfect, and we are not. We are all sinners. A perfect God can't be in the same presence as sin.

In Eden, we walked with God, and we were in communion together with Him. When our sin choice ushered in death, we could no longer remain in Eden because death and perfection are incompatible. "After he drove the man out, he placed on the east side of the garden of Eden cherubim and a flaming sword flashing back and forth to guard the way to the tree of life" (Gen. 3:24).

Even after we bit into the forbidden fruit and ushered in the knowledge of good and evil, God didn't stay on His side of the flaming sword to enjoy the perfection of Eden. He was missing His children, and to this day, He has never left us. It goes on to show in Genesis that God is still greatly involved with His kids. In Genesis 4:6–7, God was trying to guide Adam and Eve's son. "Then the Lord said to Cain, 'Why are you angry? Why is your face downcast? If you do what is right, will you not be accepted? But if you do not do what is right, sin is crouching at your door; it desires to have you, but you must rule over it.'"

The Helmet of Salvation

God continues to care about our lives, losses, feelings, and needs. Throughout the Bible and into our present day, God is still here with us, but because of sin, we can't be in Eden with Him. Therefore, God made a way—through the death and resurrection of His Son—to deal with sin's eviction notice.

We chose to allow sin to divide us from our Father and because of the chasm we created, sin had to be dealt with according to what is just and right. Not only is God perfect, He is perfectly just, and the Bible says sin comes with a penalty of death. Fortunately for us in Romans 6:23, the Bible says, "For the wages of sin is death, but the gift of God is eternal life in Christ Jesus our Lord."

Basically, what we're born into has an expiration date with eternal ramifications. It is during our time here that we have a chance to find our way back to Him. Our separation doesn't need to be eternal. He gave us a way to bridge us to Him through His Son, Jesus Christ. Because God is love, and His plan has always been to spend an eternity with us, He made a way to pay our wages of death by giving us what we can't earn—eternal life through the perfect righteousness of Christ who covered the cost of our sins. In this way, we are made perfect and free from sin.

If you are counting on your own goodness at the end of your life to earn an eternity with Jesus, this is not merely an inconvenience or frustration when you find out it's not enough. It's a decision with eternal consequences. If we question God's love for us, then we need to ask ourselves these questions, "Would I sacrifice my child in the way God sacrificed His child for people who most likely would never acknowledge or care that I did? Would I hand over my son or daughter and watch them unjustly tortured for the world we live in today?" Even while knowing most people will choose not to love Him, God gave His Son this fate because that is how much He loves us.

If God is God and can do anything, why would He not make exceptions for those who are good people even if they don't accept Christ? Doesn't living a good life mean you believe in the goodness of God?

To answer this, let's talk baseball. Some of you may be hard core fans of one team or another, but basically most people know the general rules of the game. Imagine the World Series where a runner on third hears the crack of the bat and instinctively knows it's time to run. He pushes himself to his physical limits trying to reach home. He feels movement to his left and knows he must slide into home base to have any chance of getting the run. He feels his stomach colliding with the dirt, and bits of sand and dust are gritty in his teeth. The umpire yells, "Safe!" and the whole place goes ballistic. When he opens his eyes, he realizes he is inches away from home plate; he didn't touch the base. The opposing coach throws down his cap and bolts towards the umpire. The disgusted fans can hardly be held back in their seats because of the unfairness of the call.

The umpire defends his decision because this ballplayer worked hard all week, and he had a hard time with losing his father the month before. This ball player also was nice to the umpire's grandma when she visited yesterday, and he donates a portion of his earnings to sick children. Didn't this runner deserve a little break, considering?

Did the ballplayer legitimately deserve that run? It was nice of the umpire to consider his feelings, but how long do you think this umpire will keep his job? Would he have any credibility to umpire a game again? If we expect a little more fairness and justness from our umpires, why would we expect less from our God?

If God allows sin to go unpunished, would God have any credibility? If the wages of sin are death, would we believe the truth

The Helmet of Salvation

of His Word if He bent the requirement needed to end our sin punishment? Would Christ's death even be necessary if God waved everyone into heaven and offered high fives for the good deeds we did? I don't know about you, but it bothers me greatly when someone is one hundred percent guilty of a crime and they only receive a slap on the wrist. Where is the justice in that?

Our God is the same from the beginning of time to the end of time, and He won't waiver based on our desires for leniency. Because of this, we can believe every single one of His Words to be true. We never have to doubt His way because we never have to doubt Him. Once that umpire let one ballplayer break the rules, his judgment could never be trusted again.

If you are drowning with seconds away from succumbing to the water and your only hope of survival is a life preserver that landed precious inches away from your fingertips, would your last thoughts be, "That's okay. John tried his best to throw it to me, so that's all that matters?"

A savior is meant to save. Jesus saves us conclusively and unequivocally. There is no halfway when Jesus saves or, "That's good enough." His saving is perfect, eternal, and the only way. There are no loopholes when it comes to our salvation. We either make the home run or we don't because there isn't a sliding scale for sin.

We can't say, "Well, my sin isn't as bad as that other person's sin, so I'm good," because whether you are feet away from the plate or mere inches, neither will be counted as a runner that made it home. It takes Jesus lifting us up while we are still in the prone position with our hands outstretched to bridge the distance. He carries us until our fingers connect with the pentagon-shaped rubber and only then can God clearly make the call we are, "Safe!"

The helmet of salvation is the final piece of our defensive gear, but it is through our salvation the strength of every other piece of our armor flows. Without it, as in any physical armor, the rest would be weakened in the battle for our souls. Let's honor what Jesus sacrificially gave to us and pray for the only helmet we truly need.

"Dear heavenly Father, I know I am a sinner. I know there isn't a sin I committed that you haven't seen, but you love me anyway. I can no longer hide from you, Father. I want to be rescued from the sentence of my sins, and I ask for your forgiveness. I accept Jesus' sacrifice on the cross as He took my sins and died for them. I repent of all I have done to break your heart. Please Father, keep me humble and close to you as I enter into a relationship with you today. Please keep me aware of my sinful nature and all the pitfalls of this life that will try to derail my relationship with you. I love you Father and ask for your forgiveness and the eternal blessing of never being separated from you again. In Jesus' sweet name I pray. Amen."

SWORD OF THE SPIRIT

And the sword of the Spirit, which is the word of God.
(Eph. 6:17)

Chapter 7

"TAKE THAT!"

Our final piece of armor is the only offensive piece we are given. Because it is perfect in its execution at defeating any other weapon formed against us, God's sword is the only weapon we will ever need. With this piece of armor, we can engage in our life's battles and not merely try to survive them. Our previous pieces of armor will block the weapons thrown at us, but the sword equips us to jab back at our enemy. In human terms, God's sword is equivalent to wielding a military grade weapon with GPS capabilities, but as in all things God does, He takes the most unlikely of things and transforms them into more than we could ever imagine. In this way, we can fully know our protection is from Him and not from anything we create on our own. God's weapon of choice is a book.

Whoever heard of *death by book*? It seems almost laughable, yet when we open the pages of God's Word, His message emerges as the deadliest of blades. Our sword isn't made of steel sharpened until it can split a hair. Our sword is full of words, chapters, and verses—divided into old and new—and written over a timeframe estimated to be fifteen hundred years or more. Our book, by statistical measurements, is a book of impossibilities because within that timeframe, multiple authors from every walk of life—king to peasant and prisoner to intellectual—contributed to its pages, and not one word contradicts another. Not one verse written in the first hundred years negates one verse written in the last. An author who is a king won't tell you a different truth about God than a prophet or shepherd. The likelihood of this even being achievable is mathematically mind boggling, but it all exists within the leather binding of our amazing Bible. This is God at work letting us know we can trust Him, we can trust His Word, and we possess a weapon that scares our enemy to his core. "All Scripture is God-breathed and is useful for teaching, rebuking, correcting and training in righteousness, so that the servant of God may be thoroughly equipped for every good work" (2 Tim. 3:16–17).

I bought my first Bible from Walmart®. I was in my mid-twenties when a friend of mine introduced me to a book series that piqued my interest in the teachings of the Bible. Attending church on and off most of my life, I never sat down and opened a Bible—let alone own one—to read for myself. As a teenager, I read a verse here and there during church classes when I was called upon to do so, but I read out of obligation and never let the content soak into my soul. I was punching a time clock until the hour was up.

I remember feeling weird walking into Walmart® that day. I felt like all eyes were on me as if they knew I was there to buy a Bible. I wasn't there for the typical toiletries or beach towels. I was there to pick up God's Holy Word. Did Walmart® even sell something like that? I felt like maybe I should be somewhere else purchasing the Word of God, but I was clueless as to where that place would be.

I went to the back of the store to find their books and looked up and down the shelves. I had no idea which books they shelved the Bible with, and I worried about being overwhelmed if they carried too many styles or versions. I was equally worried they wouldn't have a Bible at all. The Bible was there, and I was relieved. There weren't many choices which made it easier for me. I scooped it up and quickly headed toward the check-out. I felt so grown up in that moment.

I purchased several versions since this Bible, but my first Bible is still special to me. It was the first time I made the decision to let the Word take root in my life, and in my fumbling, unsure way of how to read it, God took me by the hand and told me it didn't matter—just read. To say it was life transforming would barely give God the glory He deserves. It took ahold of my heart and never let go. I started to read passages in the Bible which planted the seeds toward my journey of becoming a born-again believer.

During this time, I was not attending church. I never knew what I needed to do to take the helmet of salvation until another friend invited me to her church. I was nervous to go but almost instantly this church became my home. When I attended, I brought my Walmart® Bible with me and listened to the preacher preach the truth. My soul heard it clearly for the first time.

This same friend also invited me to my first Bible study. Again, I brought my Bible but panicked when the group leader asked us to turn to a certain chapter in the Bible. I looked around at everyone as they confidently turned to the right page. I felt like such a fraud being there because I wasn't even sure if the passage we were turning to was in the Old Testament or the New Testament. I closed my eyes and prayed God would help me find the right page. When I opened my Bible, it was on the exact page I needed. I looked up and smiled at God. I knew He was encouraging me to take this journey into His Word with Him. He will give us a way to understand His Word, and Satan will always try to intimidate us to never open it. God held my hand and continues to hold my hand as I enter its pages, and He will hold yours, too.

Our Bible may not physically split a hair, but its truth message is so powerful, it has divided man from man, family from family, those who don't believe from those who do believe. Thousands of Christians are martyred for their faith annually, and that number keeps rising. Wars, revolutions, protests, and crusades occurred and are occurring because of the Word of God. His Word is clear on how He asks us to live out our lives, and many in this world hate what He has to say.

God's Word isn't meant to divide us from each other, but when people want to remain lovers of sin, they will do anything to close the book on the truth and turn against those who try to open it. In Hebrews 4:12, it is written, "For the word of God is alive and active. Sharper than any double-edged sword, it penetrates even to dividing soul and spirit, joints and marrow; it judges the thoughts and attitudes of the heart."

The Bible is so transformative—and Satan despises it so much—because His Word is alive. When we open its pages, our enemy feels the stinging tip of the sword and has no choice but to retreat. The Bible splits the sin from our souls through the message of Jesus Christ and attacks the enemy who tries to blind us from this truth. Satan wants to keep the sin stain sticking to us like a freshly tarred road, and to do this, he needs us to keep the Bible closed. Our inability to see is how he morphs his lies into false truths. When people open God's Word, their blindfolds are lifted, and he is exposed. Darkness always flees in the presence of light.

We make it easy for Satan to disarm us day after day by letting our overscheduled activities, hectic mornings, tired bodies, and worn out spirits keep us from reading His Word. Our blurry vision has difficulty focusing on the words of a cereal box let alone the passages in our Bible. When we whisper to ourselves or confess to a friend we need to read our Bibles more, Satan is right there convincing us maybe we should leave it until tomorrow, the next day, or on the weekend when we will have more time and energy.

The reality is tomorrow never comes, and the weekends are as packed and overscheduled as our weekdays. Our focus is in all the wrong places. It is not by our own strength we can open God's Word and read. The strength comes from our loving God who wants to calm our bodies, soothe our minds, and feed our souls. Through His Word we are gifted the strength for another day, another meeting, another carpool, and another stretch to payday.

When we decide to come to the Bible when we feel we are ready, able, or worthy, we are relying on ourselves. We need to come to the Bible as if we are dehydrated and army crawling up a hill in desperate search of water. We don't need to come to our Bibles whole. We need to come to our Bibles broken, so His Word can make us whole. "Jesus answered, 'Everyone who drinks this water will be thirsty again, but whoever drinks the water I give them will never thirst. Indeed, the water I give them will become in them a spring of water welling up to eternal life'" (John 4:13–14).

The Bible says there will be many who are lovers of evil and will hate the truth. Those who hate the truth will spend their whole lives trying to falsify the teachings of the Bible. Over the thousands of years since its writings, there has yet to be one person to disprove the truth of God's Word. Oftentimes those who try to falsify God's claims succumb to His truths and believe. Those who hate the truth will get their wish. Their hearts will be hardened until they can no longer recognize the truth. For those who are lost, we need to have broken hearts—not judgment. We need to feel pain for those who will never know Him, who will never feel what real love and forgiveness feels like, and what real freedom tastes like. We need to pray the truth of His Word will seep into as many souls as possible.

We are not to use its pages to judge why someone else is a sinner. For every page we can quote and point out the sins of another, there are ten more pages pointing out the sins of us. The truth spoken in the Bible is for everyone. The sins written in the Bible are all of ours. The need for Jesus is the only truth we should be sharing because the words of the Bible were not written to give us permission to be the judge and jury of other's lives. We are all capable of turning its pages and reading the sins we've committed.

Jesus is the only one worthy to judge, but he didn't come to condemn us—He came to save us. If this is true, why do we feel the need to condemn each other? When we use the Bible to judge another person, we ultimately point people away from God's message by altering the weapon meant to protect into a weapon meant to hurt. When we do this, we will be held responsible for the outcome.

The Bible is a message of love, but it is not neutral in its execution of God's Word. It doesn't just offer warm and fuzzy feelings, and we aren't meant to read it, close its pages, and not be transformed as we go about our day. God is love, and His Word is love, but love sometimes brings a call to action—a call to make a change. The Bible disciplines us and points out our sins not to chastise us or give reasons why we are so unlovable. The Bible is to save us and give us the life God so desires for us to have. Even while living in a world run by a landlord who wants us to experience anything but peace and joy on this side of heaven, our God shows us the true meaning of joy and peace through our Lord and Savior, Jesus Christ. There are parts of the Bible people have great difficulty agreeing with, but God isn't asking us to agree with Him. He is asking us to trust Him. He is asking us to understand that as our Father His ways are best, and He would never steer us wrong.

Sword of The Spirit

If you have a young child or observed one in a grocery store, you've witnessed how persistent a child is when wanting to go in the opposite direction of their parent. They yank on their parent's hand, scream and pull, and try to use their little bodies to force mom or dad to change directions. They don't have the height perspective their parent has and can't understand if their parent let go, they would run headfirst into an oncoming cart. We may not agree with God's ways or understand fully why the Bible tells us to do or not to do certain things, but we need to trust His Word is there to guide us, protect us, and His eternal perspective allows Him to see farther than our human perspective.

The Bible also tends to bring up strong emotions in people who want to use its words to hold many Christians to task. They quote parts of Scripture to nail us to a wall. Our culture wants us to deny its content and turn our backs on its truth citing the fact even we as Christian's can't live up to the Bible's requirements. They are often lost on the fact the Bible's requirement that we live a perfect life makes it easy to nail all of humanity to a wall—not just Christians. God isn't oblivious to this truth that no one has the capability to meet all His expectations. Its message is not intended to nail us to a wall, but to point to the One who was nailed to a cross. It points to the One who suffered our fate because we could never live the sinless, perfect lives required to spend an eternity in heaven with our Father. God is well aware we could never do all of this, and He doesn't use this fact to condemn any of us. He wants us to see our need for a savior and throughout the Bible, points us to the One who lived the perfect life we couldn't and died the death of a sinner, so we could.

The Bible is meant to give us direction, wisdom, and a bar we are to be striving to reach. Even though God knows we will never reach that bar in our lifetime, our changed lives through Christ

Jesus gives us the hunger to pursue that direction anyway because we know our Savior will take us the rest of the way. In John 1:1-2, John writes, "In the beginning was the Word, and the Word was with God, and the Word was God. He was with God in the beginning." John goes on to say, "The Word became flesh and made his dwelling among us. We have seen his glory, the glory of the one and only Son, who came from the Father, full of grace and truth" (John 1:14). The Word of God became flesh through Jesus Christ, and He is our sword.

Our Bible has been burned, outlawed, outcast, denied, forbidden, mocked, ripped, jeered, and discarded throughout history, yet it remains one of the all-time bestselling books to this day. Replace any other book with that same treatment, and you can see how the Bible's popularity is almost inconceivable.

I don't enjoy cooking, so let's pretend I wrote a cookbook and upon distribution it was burned, outlawed, outcast, denied, forbidden, mocked, and discarded. If you ate my food, that wouldn't be an unfair estimate of what could possibly happen. I also can guarantee my cookbook's fate would not include becoming an all-time best seller. The reason for this is the content of its pages could easily be proven false and untrustworthy. The jig would be up quickly if you tried to prepare one of my dishes and wound up ordering pizza. What is expected in any cookbook is replicable dishes that would delight the cook and their families. The truth of my recipes would easily be debunked after you prepared your first meal.

The Bible remains a bestseller because its truth cannot be debunked even by the same people who have tried to burn and outlaw its teachings. Historically, kings and cities written of in the Bible, having no physical proof of existing, become platforms for those trying to prove the Bible's falsehood. That is until an archaeologist dig discovered the Bible was correct. Time and again, archaeological finds only prove the existence of the places and people written in the Bible. Those who pointed their finger at what they gleaned as false information now must move on to something else because today's science only backs what is already written. We were just slower in finding it. "Heaven and earth will pass away, but my words will never pass away" (Matt. 24:35). "The grass withers and the flowers fall, but the word of our God endures forever" (Isa. 40:8).

God doesn't worry about pointing fingers and questions, He welcomes every one of us to read its pages and decide for ourselves. He wants us to question, explore, and come to our own determination as to its authenticity. He isn't afraid of what we will or won't find because it has always proven itself in the end. God doesn't want us to blindly follow the Bible like Lemmings, listening to someone else telling us what it means. He wants your hands to dig into its pages and let it come alive in you. It's your sword after all.

A popular belief is the Bible is archaic and out of date. For those who never read its pages, it would be easy to assume this to be true. After all, how many other books do we reference with a copyright date of over two thousand years ago? For those of us who have read its pages, we can tell you it's applicable and on target for everything that is happening today. The Bible doesn't shy away from topics such as money, sex, integrity, wisdom, honesty, accountability, and war. These topics read like a news line in our daily paper.

How many politicians fall from grace because of a lack of integrity? How many lives are in ruins because of money or extramarital affairs? How many jobs are lost because of dishonest practices? How many times were you forced to hold your child or spouse accountable for their actions? Has there ever been a day where we haven't heard about war? There are wars within our homes, gang wars within our communities, wars within the workplace, wars against races, religions, and beliefs, and wars against countries and ideals—just to name a few.

How many times have you wanted a specific question answered such as how to deal with a difficult person, advice about raising children, how to strengthen a marriage, which job to take, wisdom on which way to turn, and which choices will lead to destruction and which will lead to freedom? Every time I open the Bible, a simple verse can change the direction of what I was thinking, convict me of what I was doing, or encourage me in the direction I should go. God's Word is alive. It's active, and it can only be activated when you open its pages.

Instead of judging its content from what you think it says, what you heard it said, or what you believe to be true, check it out for yourself and decide on your own. Don't rely solely on your pastor, your parents, or your Great Aunt Margaret on your father's side to tell you what the Bible says. God won't be upset if you enter its chapters with doubt and skepticism. He wants you to enter and decide for yourself.

To illustrate the power of the Word of God, I wrote a whole book on just eight verses. There are approximately 31,102 verses in the whole Bible.[1] The eight verses I wrote about comprise only 0.00026% of the Bible, yet they contain enough power and strength to take down the enemy of God. Can you imagine what the other 31,094 verses can do? And how is it possible not one of these verses contradicts another, can be disproven, or falter under the truth test? It is no wonder that God's Word is meant to be our sword.

If you have a Bible, where is it? Is it on a shelf, a table, or by your bed stacked under other more pressing things to read? Is it dusty, given to you by your grandma but never touched by you, or hidden under a pile of clothes with intentions to read when you have more time? I am as guilty as anyone for not reading as much as I should. Sometimes I listen to the lie that I don't have the time, I don't know where to begin, or I don't have the emotional fortitude at the moment to be convicted by its pages, so I walk past the Bible promising God I will read it tomorrow. I rationalize that He would understand because I don't have a minute to spare even to take a bathroom break let alone spend quiet time with Him. I tell God I don't want to shortchange Him by running through His verses when he deserves my undivided attention. He often reminds me the Bible was not written for His benefit. The Bible was written for mine.

Satan wants us to view the Bible as just another book and not the great warrior's weapon that it truly is. He wants us to be lulled into our day believing it's silly or overkill to carry our sword with us when all we are doing is going to work, school, or to the store. Do we need to carry a weapon into these places? As Satan celebrates our busy lives and enjoys spinning our hours into mere minutes, he rejoices when we let the whole day go by without us ever taking up the sword. How much more time would we add to our day if we opened the Bible to thwart off all those endless arrows by jabbing back at the one who is throwing them? When we run onto the battlefield without our weapon, we morph from a warrior into an unarmed victim who is trying to survive the arrows that never stop coming.

Let's arm ourselves with the best weapon that has ever been created. We need God's Word to complete our armor and fully be capable of fighting off the enemy's plans and lies. Let us pray for God to give us strength, time, and wisdom as we open His Word to defend ourselves against the enemy's schemes.

"Dear heavenly Father, thank you so much for your perfect Word. Thank you for thinking of everything and supplying us with all that we need to keep walking along with you in this life. Please give me the time, hunger, and thirst to open your Word and the strength to ignore all that the enemy is trying to make me believe is a better use of my time. I need to be immersed in your Word, studying it, and letting it seep into my spirit, so my days are uncluttered with the things that have me twisting and turning in the wind. Please give me the wisdom to understand your Word and the courage to apply your message to my daily life, so I can properly arm myself and fight off the attacks from the enemy. I need your Word to guide me in my decisions, in my relationships, in my home, and in my work. I pray for the sword of your Spirit to come to me with its blade pointing straight at my enemy. Please heavenly Father let your Word bathe me in your Son's love as I learn about my need of Him. Let me follow in the example of His life and ministry. In Jesus' precious name I pray. Amen."

THE WAR IS WON

For though we live in the world, we do not wage war as the world does. The weapons we fight with are not the weapons of the world. On the contrary, they have divine power to demolish strongholds. We demolish arguments and every pretension that sets itself up against the knowledge of God, and we take captive every thought to make it obedient to Christ. (2 Cor. 10:3–5)

CHAPTER 8

ARE YOU DRESSED FOR SUCCESS?

With each new day we are given the will to decide if we want to put on the armor of God or not. Just as we slip the shirt over our heads and legs into our pants, we have a choice as to what we dress in for the battles awaiting us. Satan watches as we layer on our clothes and searches for the opportunity to disable our gifts—so we add less to this world and not more. Satan doesn't care if your outfit matches. His only concern is if your decision for the day included being fully dressed or completely naked.

Satan recoils at the idea we can touch each other's lives in a positive and nurturing way. He forces distractive circumstances guaranteeing we will leave each other alone. He waits and observes as he eyes us to see if we left the armor at the door. By taking note of how we dress, he knows how far his plans for us will go based upon the type and amount of armor we decide to wear. Sometimes his plans are forced to be delivered in a slow, deliberate trickle, and sometimes they are a fast-moving current. It depends upon how many layers of armor we have protecting us. No shield? He knows he can make you stumble in your faith which puts you at odds with God. No belt of truth? He knows he won't need to do much to make his disguised lies seem believable. No shoes of peace? He knows you will be standing still, frightened, and confused by your dilemmas all the while feeling confident no movement forward will be taking place.

Satan knows every word of the Bible, and he knows the truth it speaks. He has more knowledge than anyone regarding the effectiveness of the armor of God because it was created to destroy him. The Bible tells us he must flee when we wear it, and he wants this truth to stay hidden. James 4:7 says, "Submit yourselves, then, to God. Resist the devil, and he will flee from you."

If you are anything like me, getting ready in the morning and out the door on time with the kids in tow is more like a mad dash than a leisurely stroll. I'm lucky to be wearing my regular clothes let alone my spiritual ones. It makes it easy to forget the importance of taking time for God to dress us. Sometimes I say a quick prayer or read a Scripture verse, but most of the time my interruptions are just too great. When the interruptions do come, I wind up putting God on hold.

If you received a call from your mother, friend, or even a stranger at the car dealership informing you your car was ready for pick up, how long would you put them on hold to answer another call, or hush a talkative child, before you returned to your conversation? You most likely would only make them wait a few seconds. What does it look like to put God on hold? When you've been interrupted while praying or reading His Word, how long did it take for you to reconnect with God after your mind suddenly shifted focus to life's nagging demands—a few minutes, a few days, or a year?

I am guilty of putting my Father on hold and suddenly looking around at my life wondering where and when it all started to go off track. Why am I feeling so empty and alone suddenly? The answer is always the same. During these complicated and chaotic times, I realize I left the phone off the hook, the hold button is flashing, and the receiver is still in my hand. I left God waiting.

Putting God on hold as we wrestle with our daily demands is like building a house of snow in the Midwest during the winter. As we diligently work to create a comfortable dwelling, the temporary winter weather supports our endeavors by supplying the snow that fortifies our walls. It's when spring comes, and our homes are washed away in the blazing sun, we recognize our efforts and hearts were focused on a season that didn't last forever. This is similar to when we build our kingdoms in this temporary world because God's Son will come. "Then I saw 'a new heaven and a new earth,' for the first heaven and the first earth had passed away, and there was no longer any sea" (Rev. 21:1).

When we take God off hold, we put our trust in the one who sent His Son and gave His armor to defend us from the temporaries of a broken world. When we keep Him on hold, we give audience to Satan's lies. Satan fears the armor we wear and when he is under attack, he is prepared to use every trick to convince us to undress. He stretches out his hand toward the path before us and disguises our every day as not needing a spiritual protection. He points out what is ahead to distract us from the storms trailing not far behind.

If we give him an audience and not God, we can be easily convinced to strip off one piece of armor at a time and toss it over our shoulders because we believe the lie it is not needed. We step over our protection and run headlong toward the cliffs. We dismantle and shed the one thing protecting us and giving us vision to see what dangers are before us. When we blindly take the path of our desires without God's armor—one foot and then the other—it's not until the jaws snap behind us do we grasp we've been eaten by our deceiver. God said even in this place, He can still reach us. Will you reach out for Him?

I believe a lot of people view our earthly time as an uphill marathon in the dead of summer. As we trudge along—dragging our aching bodies up the hill with sweatbands soaked until they can no longer hold another molecule of liquid—we picture God on the sidelines cheering us on, holding up signs, and encouraging us to keep on going. We decided the race is on our effort alone, and God is only there to be a great source of moral support by offering us towels every so often to wipe away the salty sweat from our eyes.

This vision limits God's great power and love for us. He is not on the sidelines cheering us on. He is right next to us running the race with us. He is the cool breeze tickling the backs of our necks and resetting our hot, worn out bodies. He is the thirst-quenching water to replenish what we lost, and His Son will carry us the rest of the way. He floods us with His Holy Spirit which allows us to clearly hear the truths of His Word, and our steps are no longer heavy but confident and light. He is that caressing, guiding voice telling us which way to turn and which pitfalls to avoid. After running our race with our faith and our trust firmly planted in Him, God is at the finish line embracing us and declaring, "'Well done, good and faithful servant!'" (Matt. 25:23).

The purpose of our life's journey is to find our way back to our Father. Sin made us lose our way in the woods, and we need His Son's lamp light to find our way back. When we claim Earth as our forever home, we ignore all the teachings in the Bible cautioning us to not stockpile things in this world. When we do, we forget our true purpose and soften the truth of our sin forming a chasm between here and our one true home in heaven. Matthew 6:19–21 says, "Do not store up for yourselves treasures on earth, where moths and vermin destroy, and where thieves break in and steal. But store up for yourselves treasures in heaven, where moths and vermin do not destroy, and where thieves do not break in and steal. For where your treasure is, there your heart will be also."

The War is Won

Our sins take the beautiful things God planned for each of our lives and throws them into the fire. Sin is a dirty smudge on our face we can't wipe away no matter how hard we try. The Bible needs us to eradicate these smudges, so we can be in His presence. No matter what solvent we use, what loofah we buy, or what soap we try, the smudges will remain. The Bible says we need to be made perfect and without blemish to be with Him.

In our sin, we are standing at the bottom of the deepest valley while looking up longingly at the home we yearn for. The promises of the Bible are at the peak of a mountain top, and we acknowledge we will never be able to reach them on our own. The wonderful thing is God already knew this and never expected us to reach high enough to grab the Bible from where we stood. Jesus came to bridge this divide and took the promises of the Bible from the peak of the mountain and put them directly into our hands.

Jesus tells us He will make us perfect and clean and His blood is powerful enough to wash off every smudge. When God sees us, He will see us through the perfection of His Son. Put both of your hands into His, and He will set you free. First John 1:9 tells us, "If we confess our sins, he is faithful and just and will forgive us our sins and purify us from all unrighteousness." Our armor is impenetrable with the assurances of our mighty God. Will you choose to wear it and if not, what are some of the reasons why?

I have friends who cite the happenings of this world as their reason for not believing in a loving God and made the choice to keep the armor off their body. If God loves us, how can He let such terrible things happen?

Imagine someone gave you a gift. This gift was an exquisite, one of a kind, perfectly crafted porcelain doll. The gift was placed lovingly into your hands and after inspecting it for a few seconds, you threw it onto the ground smashing it into a million pieces. As the bits of porcelain scattered across the floor, you point at the one who gave you this gift and blame them for it breaking.

This is what happens when we blame God for the hurt, pain, and disease of this world. He lovingly created Eden and gently placed this gift into our hands. It was perfect, tailored to meet our every need, and neither death nor pain could touch us. By choosing sin, we smashed this world into a million little pieces and broke the perfection God designed, meanwhile blaming Him for ushering in all the pain and suffering we experience. God is perfect and righteous and incapable of creating a world as broken as ours, but in His great love, He didn't abandon us here but chose to live among us. I'm always amazed that we serve a God so great He chose to become a man to save us from ourselves. Selfless is too small of a word to describe the loving God we serve.

Satan would like for us to keep blaming God. He loves when we see God as our enemy and not him. This is a practical way to blind us from the truth of his plans and keep the armor hanging useless in a closet. Satan would rather see us walking our dog wearing only a t-shirt and underwear. That would give the neighbors something to talk about. They may whisper to each other and question the state of our minds stepping out in public without wearing pants.

This is how Satan sees us when we wear maybe one or two pieces of God's armor, and we step out onto his playing field. He is pointing and laughing because he knows our minds aren't fully believing the truth of God's Word since we came to the spiritual battle so unprepared. He discerns we came to the battle silently thinking, "I've got this," "It's not that big of a deal," "I don't see any battle. That's silly!" "Come on, you are crazy, no one is attacking me." I wish it wasn't true, and we weren't in a spiritual battle. I wish there wasn't someone like Satan, but there is. Every day we are exposed to unbelievable evil in our world, and evil didn't materialize out of nowhere. There is an author of this evil, and if we are in the presence of it daily, why aren't we more prepared?

We train soldiers to be ready to fight, and they train to be adequately prepared for any type of attack they may face. They are trained to spot their enemy and always be aware of their location to avoid any surprises. Most of the time, we don't even acknowledge our enemy even exists. He is free to do whatever serves his purpose with little interruption from us.

Our spiritual enemy's only mission is to see our name is not written in the Lamb's Book of Life, so God loses out on another one of His children. We are allowing this to occur in droves. His agenda is to hurt God by hurting us, and he is winning. Satan wants us to rebel in the same way as he tricked Adam and Eve to rebel in the garden of Eden. He is trying to train and recruit soldiers obedient only to him, not soldiers who are obedient to God. Satan's tactic is to keep us sheep believing he is the shepherd.

When we are sheep following his voice, we are less likely to become the protected warriors of God. He scans to make sure that most people are naked and flinches when he spots those of us who are fully dressed in God's armor. Today, how many people do you think he sees naked compared to those who are fully protected? I think Satan sees a lot of people walking their dog in their underwear.

Wherever you are right now, picture in a flash all that is surrounding you is gone. Your chair, your bed, your home, your backyard trees, the grass, and the new carpet you bought vanished. All you invested your time, effort, and money into to make your life comfortable has now crumpled and disappeared. The echoes of your thoughts are all you have left. In front of you stands Jesus, and He asks you one question, "Did you live today for me, or did you live today for you?" How would you answer?

This thought came to me as I was sitting in church today. I felt Him asking, "Crista, who are you living for?" I was ashamed in what my answer would be. How many countless hours have I spent on social media instead of reading and protecting myself with the sword of God's Word? How much time have I spent fixing, repairing, and caring for the things I bought now stripped away in the blink of an eye? How many thoughts were occupied by worry and fear instead of God? How many few, precious seconds have I devoted my life to furthering God's kingdom compared to furthering my own? At church today I felt utterly naked, and my answer would have been utterly miserable. He reminded me of who I am living for and helped redirect my attention to what truly matters. He reminded me to wear His armor.

God doesn't expect us to run over each other trying to outdo our works for Him. Sometimes, it's how we are living for Him in our own households that matters most. Are we creating a home that honors God through the things we say, the things we watch, and the time we give to Him? Are we making sure our own children, family, and friends understand the importance of being fully clothed in God's armor, so they too are protected from the author of lies? Are we nurturing a home so our children— whom God entrusted to us—can go forward and be kingdom workers for Him? Some of us are called on missions to preach His Word across the globe. Some of us are called to be missionaries right where we are planted which includes our homes, our communities, and in our places of work.

The full armor of God is vital if we are to live out our lives intentionally. We need to be protected, so we can in turn guide those toward wearing the proper protection. As in the instructions given when taking a flight, in case of an emergency and the oxygen masks are released, put the mask on yourself first before you give it to your child. If you are incapacitated, you are of no use to anyone else. Make sure the armor of God is fully fitted on your body before you try to help someone else understand how to put it on theirs. Satan wants you to fail at touching a life, so if you choose to go without God's armor, he will not only win against you, but he will win against those you are able to reach.

Even the smallest of beings is precious in the eyes of God. Recently, I visited a pet store and asked the person working if I could please hold a guinea pig. I never held a guinea pig before, and it has been my heart's longing for many months to have one. I thought I would hold his sweet, furry body to observe his temperament and decide whether a guinea pig would make a good pet for our family.

As the employee reached into his enclosure, the guinea pig ran as fast as he could to escape the grasping fingers and tried desperately not to be caught. Eventually, through the tenacity of the store clerk, he was captured. She gently held him close to her chest with his nose facing her chin. As she stroked his fur and scratched his head, his body became limp and plump and loosened until it filled her cupped hand. His little eyes closed letting her know how much he appreciated her touch. I rubbed his white, little nose, and I couldn't wait to hold him. When she handed him over to me, it was love. What a sweetie. I thought of God in that moment and how amazingly creative He is to design such a wonderful little life.

You are so precious in the eyes of God. You didn't come here by happenstance, and neither did that adorable, cowlicked, ball of fur. Even something as simple as a teacup had a designer. My teacups aren't terribly expensive and were mass-produced, but I still love their creamy color and delicate stature. A pale, pink flower is painted on the front, and it has a swirl design in the pottery at the rim and on the handle to give it a little more personality. These teacups aren't rare, but their value is in what I behold. They make me smile.

For me to own those teacups in my cabinet, someone within the company had to decide they needed to exist. Someone chose their shape and color, the design of the flower, how many and at what intervals the swirls would take place, how tall and how open the cup would be, and how much liquid it would hold. Someone took great care in deciding on the details of this teacup and the design of the saucer it would rest upon.

If something as ordinary as a teacup had to go through such a design and production process, how much more of a world-class designer would be needed to bring the human body, thinking mind, and beating heart into existence? What would the cost and value be for people who know how to love as compared to a teacup that doesn't live, breathe, or think? At what price would the designer be willing to pay to save His creation from destruction? He would give up everything, and He did. He asked His Son to leave heaven and be killed on a cross. You are of great value to God, and He gave up everything so you could be armed, clothed in His love, and protected from what is seeking to keep you in the dark.

We need to take care of our physical bodies by feeding, hydrating, cleansing, exercising, clothing and bringing them to doctors and dentists for preventive care and ongoing medical attention. We take such good care of the physical body, yet we are unaware of how neglected and vulnerable we have let our spiritual selves become. In the way we take care of our physical selves, we need to also take care of our spiritual selves.

When we feel the pain of a broken bone, we stop everything and race to the emergency room for care. When we take a pan out of a hot oven and accidentally make contact, we instantly pull our hand back and away from the heat. Why don't we do the same for our spiritual selves? When our marriages are breaking and cracking down to the marrow, why aren't we wrapping ourselves in Christ's armor for protection? When the path we are choosing is leading us into the fire, why aren't we praying to our Father to clothe us in His truth and light?

Clothe your body to stay warm from the elements, but also clothe your spirit with the armor of God. Make the enemy flee instead of allowing him the opportunity to work overtime ensuring you will never be free. Without God's protection, we are inviting our enemy at our table to eat with our families, tempt us in our jobs, and walk beside our children.

For me, the armor of God Scripture is written like a battle cry. I can picture all of God's Christian soldiers in the locker room listening to God giving His instructions before we go out into battle. He tells us what is needed, who our enemy is, and how to end up at the end still standing. Let me pray over you as you go forward and join your faith shield with mine and clothe your body in the only clothes that matter.

"Dear heavenly Father, I pray specifically and fervently for this precious child of yours. I pray their journey into learning more about your armor allows them to feel the comfort and security of your covering, and it becomes as familiar to them as putting on their socks and shoes. I pray the enemy's temptations and schemes will be made visible in the light as you bestow your wisdom and discernment regarding his plans. I pray for heightened senses as they see and feel your love in the many ways you are trying to show it to them. I pray for growth and humbleness as they put their arms into the robe of Christ's righteousness and fully understand the cost paid to make it available.

I pray when given eyes to see, they will make the choice to leave each day fully dressed, so when the enemy tries to attack, they will have your full strength to keep them standing. I pray for blessings over their family and friends as they observe your child walking in Christ's shoes of peace and ask where they got them. I pray for boldness to tell their family and friends about the enemy's schemes as we grow into a protected community wearing the full armor of God.

Thank you, Lord, for touching the life of this precious person whom you love so much. Thank you for loving us unconditionally and sending a Savior who will one day judge the world, throw down our enemy, and usher in His reign which allows us to live where your Son will shine forever and ever. I pray all of this in Jesus' wonderful and Holy name. Amen

NOTES

Chapter 4

1. "Footwear Industry Statistics – Statistic Brain." Statistic Brain Research Institute, publishing as Statistic Brain. 13 Aug. 2016; see http://www.statisticbrain.com/footwear-industry-statistics/.

2. See http://www.ucmp.berkeley.edu/education/explorations/tours/geotime/guide/billion.html.

Chapter 7

1. "The 66 Books of the Bible." Blue Letter Bible. Accessed 18 Oct, 2016. https://www.blueletterbible.org/study/misc/66books.cfm

GROUP BIBLE STUDY
SPECIAL PRICING

The Armor of God

+

The Workbook Companion for The Armor of God

Please email interest to:

books@plantedinhim.com

NEWSLETTER

Sign up to receive a ***once a month*** newsletter full of updates on new book releases, giveaways, discounts, and encouragement.

cristacrawford.com/newsletter

ABOUT THE AUTHOR

Crista Crawford is an imperfect Christian writing about her perfect God. She discovered the power of praying each piece of armor into her life after stumbling through multiple trials only to fall face-first without it. She is a wife, mother, and stepmother who feels incredibly blessed sharing life with these amazing people. Crista is an Emerson Excellence in Teaching Award winner and has a Master of Science in Speech-Language Pathology and a Master of Arts in Educational studies with Reading Emphasis. She has over twenty years' experience as a Speech-Language Pathologist and forty-plus years learning what grace and forgiveness really mean.

Please visit Crista on Goodreads or her Author's Facebook page and let her know your thoughts on *The Full Armor of God*.

Our stories are meant to be shared because our testimonies carry the power to light the path for those who are still struggling in the dark. What we overcome may be the foundation for others to use as their steppingstone.

Let's Stay Connected!

Website: - cristacrawford.com
Facebook Page: - facebook.com/CCrawfordAuthor
Twitter: - @CCrawfordAuthor
Instagram: - ccrawfordauthor
Goodreads: bit.ly/cristacrawford

www.ingramcontent.com/pod-product-compliance
Lightning Source LLC
Chambersburg PA
CBHW070625300426
44113CB00010B/1661